Better Homes & Gardens®

Celebrate

Volume 7

contents

begin

spring

food

summer

boo!

easy does it

Let your talents shine, even when you're short on time!

Better Homes & Gardens
Celebrate
Volume 7

MEREDITH CONSUMER MARKETING
Consumer Marketing Product Director: Heather Sorensen
Consumer Marketing Product Manager: Tami Perkins
Consumer Products Marketing Manager: Wendy Merical
Business Manager: Diane Umland
Senior Production Manager: Al Rodruck

WATERBURY PUBLICATIONS, INC.
Editorial Director: Lisa Kingsley
Creative Director: Ken Carlson
Associate Editor: Tricia Bergman
Associate Design Director: Doug Samuelson
Production Assistant: Mindy Samuelson
Contributing Editor: Sue Banker
Contributing Copy Editor: Gretchen Kauffman
Contributing Proofreader: Peg Smith

BETTER HOMES & GARDENS® MAGAZINE
Editor in Chief: Stephen Orr
Executive Editor: Oma Blaise Ford
Managing Editor: Gregory H. Kayko
Creative Director: Jennifer D. Madara
Senior Deputy Editor, Food and Entertaining: Nancy Wall Hopkins

MEREDITH NATIONAL MEDIA GROUP
President: Tom Harty

MEREDITH CORPORATION
Chairman and Chief Executive Officer: Stephen M. Lacy

In Memoriam: E.T. Meredith III (1933–2003)

get ready to shine!

Whether you want to spruce up your space, host the best get-together EVER, or make your yard come alive with creativity, *Better Homes & Gardens®* *CELEBRATE* can help!

In these pages you'll explore exciting color palettes. You'll learn fun crafting techniques as well as how to create appealing decor for your home and yard. Many of the projects make wonderful gifts! Plus you'll discover delicious recipes and party tips that will win accolades like never before.

When it comes to holidays or special events, you'll be armed with awesome projects and recipes to celebrate the happiest New Year to the most haunting Halloween and all the special days in between.

So let your enthusiasm and creativity SHINE! *CELEBRATE* will be your guide every step of the way.

Wishing you the best of days,

begin

NEW YEAR, NEW DECOR
Bask in the memories of year-end celebrations while looking ahead to new beginnings. Start with fresh DIY treasures for your home.

Destination Delights

Vintage vacation postcards recall treasured vacation memories any time of the year while personalizing decor along the way.

MAP IT OUT

Atlas pages spark conversation at the dining table. To make a place mat, carefully remove two facing pages and tape them together on the back. If using for guests, use pages from states that are meaningful to them. For reusable place mats, laminate them at a copy shop.

SHOW OFF

Carry out the theme with original or copies of vintage postcards positioned under clear glass plates and around the tabletop. Display the backs of those with interesting artwork, stamps, or handwriting.

HOMETOWN CHARM

Metal-rim key tags act as miniature frames for map segments
that relate to each guest. For circular tags, use a circle maker
to cut out the shape from a map, atlas, or printout. Punch a
hole at the top to align with the one on the tag, attach with glue
stick, and tie to the glass stem with string.

DESTINATION COLLECTION

Pair travel souvenirs, such as these ceramic dogs, with a framed
enlargement of a vintage postcard from a special vacation
destination. Mount the enlargement on paper cut from atlas
pages or a map to border the image. Frame the meaningful
treasure and display it with your souvenir collection.

WORLDLY VASE

A section of a map, wrapped around a cylindrical vase, adds playful personalization. Hot-glue jute and rope trim around the vase for nautical appeal.

MEMORY MAGNETS

Relive your favorite travels every day with postcard refrigerator magnets. Print reduced copies of postcards on white cardstock to fit adhesive-backed business card magnet sheets.

Treasured Hearts

Wood shapes and junk-drawer finds come together to make one-of-a-kind heart decorations to love year-round.

WALL FLOWER

This fun textural wall heart shares hugs and kisses long after Valentine's Day has passed.

WHAT YOU NEED

decorative pieces, such as "x" tile
    spacers, plastic rings, washers,
    o-rings, wire, studs, wood letters,
    buttons, and button forms
wood heart plaque with hanger
super glue
white primer spray paint
white spray paint
acrylic paint in desired colors
paintbrush
clear coat sealer

WHAT YOU DO

1. Gather decorative pieces, as shown in Photo A, to decorate the wood heart plaque.

2. Remove the hanger from the wood heart. Decide on placement of decorative pieces and glue in place. Let the glue dry. Remove any excess glue.

3. In a well-ventilated work area, spray-paint the decorated heart with white primer as shown in Photo B; let dry. Apply a coat of white spray paint; let dry.

4. Paint desired details using acrylic paint as shown in Photos C–F. Let the paint dry.

5. Spray heart with a coat of clear coat and let dry. Replace the hanger.

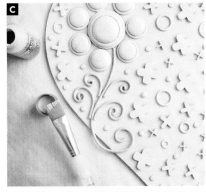

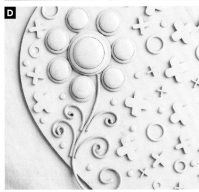

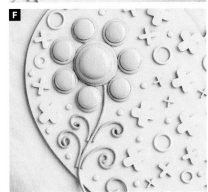

LOTSA LOVE FRAME

Make your own initial photo frames in all your favorite colors. Start with an unfinished wood filigree frame, heart, and letter, all available at crafts stores. Paint each piece; let dry. Attach the pieces with instant glue and insert a photo in the frame.

CIRCLE OF LOVE
VASE BASE

A mini flat wreath form makes the perfect base for this sweet trivet. Paint large and small wooden hearts and circles and let dry. Use instant glue to attach the large hearts to the base with the small hearts and circles on top to create the desired arrangement.

CUTE COASTERS

Indoor-outdoor paint gives these little beauties a layer of water protection. Use waterproof glue to adhere small wood pieces, including hearts, to a 4-inch wood circle. Group the pieces close together so glasses will sit on the coaster without tipping. Attach the wood circle to a laser-cut heart. Spray-paint the coaster with two coats of indoor-outdoor spray paint, allowing it to dry between coats. Spray with two coats of waterproof clear sealer and let dry.

Put a Spin on It

Kick off the year with clever home accents that breathe new life into vinyl records and their jackets.

STORAGE FOR A SONG

Plain 12-inch hatboxes get a designer look with the help of a record and its jacket. To make the jacket hatbox cover, carefully cut the jacket along the folds. Trace a circle onto the back side of the jacket cover piece, slightly smaller than the lid, using a plate, bowl, or other round object as a pattern; cut out. Attach the cutout to the lid using strong glue stick or double-sided tape. Tie a piece of color-coordinated fabric around the bottom of the hatbox. For the record lid, measure and mark the center of the hatbox lid. Use an awl to poke a hole where marked. Attach the record to the lid using adhesive for paper and plastic. Thread the bolt from a knob through the hole and secure with a nut. If desired, cover the base of the hatbox with fabric.

FAVORITE PICK

Pay tribute to the music that tugs at your heartstrings. Vinyl record frames are just the ticket to flaunt your favorites. For an unexpected accent, use colorful guitar picks to create a cascade of flowers that trail from the framed jacket cover to the album. Before gluing in place, brush each pick with a light coat of white acrylic paint, allowing the color to show through. When dry, arrange and glue the picks to the frame glass, using the photograph as inspiration. Use black buttons for the flower centers.

HIGH NOTE

Attach inexpensive 45 records to a plain wood or metal coatrack to give it something to croon about. Arrange the vinyl 45s, which you can score secondhand, around the hooks. Secure the records to the rack and each other with heavy-duty adhesive.

BEST-HITS BACKGROUND

Make a wall sing with 45s arranged in a bold polka dot effect. Use tiny nails or poster putty to attach records to the wall. Once the first straight row is up, shift the next row so the shapes nest as shown or create your own design, such as flowers or random dots.

Hats Off to St. Pat's Day

Leprechaun hats, big and small, set the stage for a celebratory day.

CENTER OF ATTENTION

When March 17 rolls around, celebrate St. Patrick's Day with a grand, yet easy, centerpiece. Place a bowl inside a green hat and fill with floral foam; add water. Arrange short flowers in the hat, then add taller stalks as accents.

LUCKY JARS

Share St. Patrick's Day wishes with goodie jars dressed in green. Small hats, available at crafts stores and costume shops, make fun jar toppers. Trim each one with a band of ribbon, a shamrock pin, and a sprig of artificial flowers.

Paper Piecing

Capture the look of quilting (without a single stitch!) using patterned papers in fresh hues.

TULIP TIME

Freshen up a wall with a delightful floral design in spring hues. This stunning piece is crafted on a lightweight ceiling tile that mimics the look of an expensive frame. Use a 1½-inch square-maker punch (cutting some in half diagonally) and the patterns on page 152 to create the pieces, using the photograph as a guide. Use strong glue stick to adhere the tulip design to a 10-inch square of white cardstock, leaving a ½-border. Back the design with a 12-inch square of colored cardstock. If using the same style ceiling tile, the design can be bordered in evenly spaced 1½-inch squares. The design can easily be adapted to other styles of tile.

Begin

NOTABLE NOTES

Make someone's day with a sentiment written on a handmade card. A perfect scrap project, this card works up quickly using 1- and ½-inch square-maker punches. For the triangles, use scissors to cut squares corner to opposite corner. Use a glue stick to attach the pieces to a 4½×9-inch piece of white cardstock folded in half. Start in one corner of the card front, leaving a ¼-inch border. Add the pieces in rows, keeping them aligned straight.

PRETTY DRESDEN PLATE

A quilting classic, the Dresden plate design, is simple yet showy. Blend your favorite colors and patterns to jazz up your table. Use the pattern on page 152 to cut 16 wedge shapes and tape together on the back. To make the mat waterproof, laminate it at a copy shop.

DOOR DECOR

A woodchip key brings interest to an entry door. Whether you choose a key, an initial, or other shape, you can personalize the "wreath" using your favorite colors, patterns, and theme. The ever-popular wedding ring quilt pattern covers a 12-inch wreath form to back the shape. Use a marking pen to draw "stitch lines" around the edges of the ring.

HEXAGON HOLDER

A glass vase gets a pretty facelift with the addition of a lovely paper band. Use a hexagon maker to punch several shapes from coordinating papers. Trim a few of the shapes in half to place along the top edge, leaving a narrow border of the background paper. Use a strong glue stick to adhere the shapes to a strip of cardstock cut to fit cylinder; leave equal narrow borders between shapes. Use double-sided tape to attach the band to the cylinder.

Sweet Valentines

DOILY POCKETS

With all their characteristic holes, doilies are perfect for handstitching. Using 4–6 layers for both the front and back, stitch the layers together (leaving the top open) using embroidery floss and running (page 152) and/or buttonhole stitches. Tuck a plastic treat bag into the pocket, fill with small candies, and close with a twist tie.

PLAYING CUPID

Colorful corrugated paper gives these sturdy heart-shape pockets eye-popping texture. Paper straws make easy arrows. Trace around a 5-inch heart-shape cookie cutter on corrugated paper and cut out. Fold heart on the diagonal and punch holes through both layers in the center about ½ inch from fold. Using pinking shears, cut another heart from corrugated paper in a contrasting color, making it about ¼ inch larger on all sides. Apply crafts tape along the sides of small heart (not top), center on large heart, and attach. For arrow, trace and cut out two heads and two tails from solid cardstock. Tape tail pieces to paper straw. Fringe tail. Thread straw through holes of top heart. Attach arrowhead to straw with tape. Fill heart with small candies. Seal top with glue dots.

STUCK ON YOU

The coloring craze comes to Valentine's Day. Draw or print out simple designs on full sheets of sticker paper; cut out hearts from the paper. Color in the designs as desired and press the sticker onto a colored bag. Fold over the top and punch two holes side by side. Insert a few sweet treats, thread the holes with string, and tie closed.

PEEKABOO PACKAGES

Closed they're graphic patterned bookmarks. Open they reveal two surprises: a sweet treat and a hidden colorful heart shape. To make a treat holder, cover work area with newspaper. Glue together two pieces of paper, one patterned and one solid color, using spray adhesive. Trace the pattern on page 152; cut out. Trace around the pattern onto the solid-color side and cut out using a straightedge and crafts knife. Crease the center from top to bottom using a ruler and bone folder. Apply double-sided tape along the left side (below flap) and bottom of the card, then firmly press along tape to create pocket. Fold top flap closed and punch a hole in the upper right corner. Add treat, thread narrow ribbon through the hole, and tie.

SWEET SENTIMENTS

A handmade Valentine warms the heart. To transform a plain notecard, open it on a cutting board and use a crafts knife to cut five horizontal 2-inch-long slits ½ inch apart. Carefully weave ribbon through the slits, taping the ends to the inside of the card. Cut a piece of cardstock to fit the inside cover of the card and glue it over the back side of the weaving. Hot-glue two ribbon pieces along the card opposite the weaving as shown. Write a message in the card and put a treat bag holding a few small candies inside as a bonus.

spring

THE COLORS UNFOLD

As the earth and creatures awaken, be inspired to breathe creativity and color into your surroundings one project at a time.

Loose Threads

Embroidery threads in a rainbow of colors put a fresh spin on springtime decor.

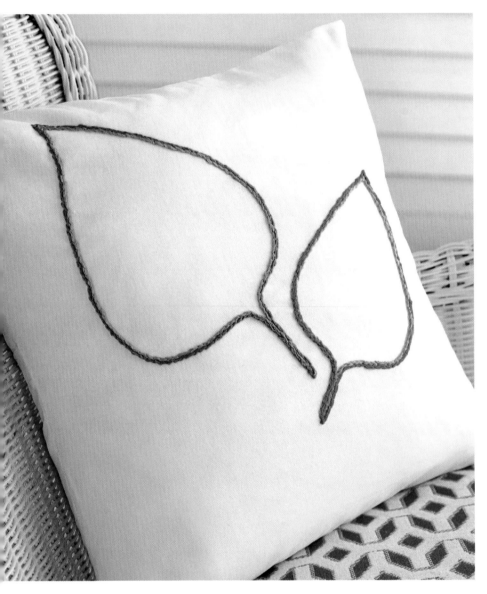

LEAF-SHAPE PILLOW

A sunflower leaf was used to create this pattern, but any leaf will do. Try hosta, maple, or linden.

WHAT YOU NEED
leaves
½ yard white outdoor fabric
pillow form
water soluble fabric pen
embroidery hoop
embroidery floss and needle

WHAT YOU DO
1. Gather your supplies as shown in Photo A.
2. Cut two pieces of fabric an inch longer and wider than pillow form. On one piece, trace leaves using a water soluble marking pen as shown in Photo B.
3. Using the embroidery hoop, floss, and needle, begin stitching around the leaf shape. We used a split stitch: Start with one straight stitch, then bring your needle up through the underside of the fabric to split the strands of floss in the original stitch as shown in Photo C. Continue to stitch around the entire shape.
4. Using embroidery floss a shade lighter, create a thicker outline by placing a second row of split stitches just inside the original as shown in Photo D. Follow the same instructions as in Step 3. Repeat for all leaf shapes on your pillow top. When finished, sew the embellished square to the plain square to create a pillow cover.

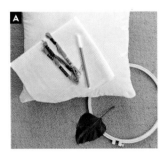
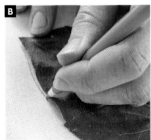

COLOR-WRAPPED POSIES

Choose your favorite hues of embroidery floss to make this vibrant art piece that enlivens any space. Use a 12-inch square of ⅜-inch-thick birch for the light background. Drill holes around the edges every ½ inch, leaving a ½-inch border; sand smooth. Use a pencil to lightly draw 2½-, 3-, and 4-inch-diameter offset circles for the tall flower and 2½- and 3-inch circles for the short flower. Starting in a center circle, hammer in small brass brads approximately ½ inch apart. Outline all circles in this manner. Hammer in brads for the stems and leaves. To wrap brads with embroidery floss, start with a flower center. Tie the floss end to one brad. To create a spoke effect, wind floss around the opposite brad, then to the one to the left of the first brad. Continue winding the floss in this manner to complete the center. Knot the floss on the last brad and cut off the tail. For the circles, stems, and leaves, simply wind floss around the outside of the brads. For the border, thread a needle with floss and stitch through the drilled holes.

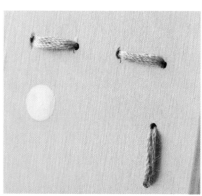

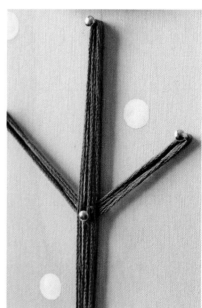

RAINBOW NEST

*So cheery, this playful nest gets it color
from combining four different skeins of
variegated embroidery floss.*

WHAT YOU NEED
balloon
glass
tape
decoupage medium
soft paintbrush
four skeins variegated embroidery floss
scissors

WHAT YOU DO
1. Blow up a balloon to the desired size and
tie off. Knot down, tape the balloon to a
glass as shown in Photo A.
2. Use a soft paintbrush to apply
decoupage medium to the top half of the
balloon as shown in Photo B.
3. Wrap one skein of floss around the
balloon as shown in Photo C; top with more
decoupage medium as shown in Photo D.
Continue working in this manner until all
four skeins are used as shown in Photo E.
4. Apply a final thick coat of decoupage
medium as shown in Photo F. Let dry until all
decoupage medium is clear and floss is dry
and hard to the touch as shown in Photo G.
(This may take a couple of days.)
5. Remove the balloon from the glass.
Cut off the knotted end of the balloon as
shown in Photo H and carefully remove
the balloon from the nest. Fill the nest with
paper shred and candy.

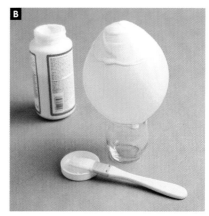

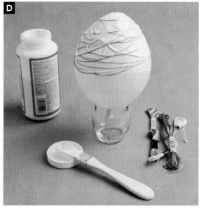

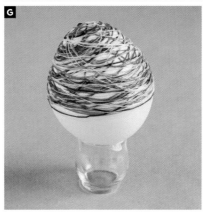

Extraordinary Eggs

Permanent marking pens transform matte porcelain eggs into lasting works of art.

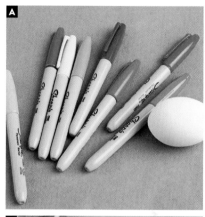

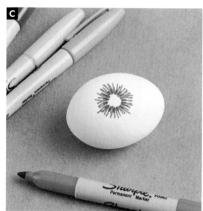

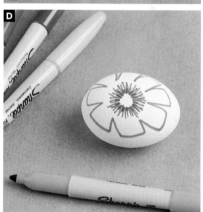

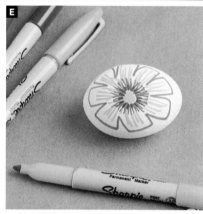

SPRING BLOOMS

For bold floral designs, use the shape of the egg to guide your drawing. Gather desired colors of permanent marking pens as shown in Photo A. To make the flower, start by making a short-spoke circle approximately the size of a dime as shown in Photo B. Add longer spokes with a slightly different color as shown in Photo C. Use the egg shape to draw the flower petals as shown in Photo D. Using a color contrasting to the flower center, draw longer spokes into each petal as shown in Photo E. Draw a few sprigs of greenery and leaves around flower as shown in Photo F. Add tiny flowers as shown in Photos G and H.

DOODLE TIME

Create one-of-a-kind patterns on porcelain eggs, then dip-dye them for an overall kiss of color. Mix a cup of vinegar and a few drops of food coloring to dye drawn-on egg. Place egg on a spoon, immerse into dye, remove, and let dry on a paper towel-covered disposable plate.

INITIAL EGGS

Make Easter breakfast extra special with personalized eggs at everyone's place at the table. Adhere a sticker letter to the front of an egg. Use marking pens in a variety of colors to draw lines from the center of the letter outward as shown in the photograph. Add small dots to the ends of some of the lines. Remove the sticker to reveal the initial.

PLAID-CLAD

Striking and super easy to do, this egg packs a colorful punch. Scribble zigzags in different widths around the egg in both directions to create a plaid effect.

Sticks and Stones

Make trendy home accents with inspiration from Mother Nature.

TAKE FLIGHT

Gather fallen branches (or purchase them at a crafts store) to create a delightful airy display. Center a glass vase or hurricane on a log slice from a crafts store. Outline the container base with a pencil, then measure out 1 inch and draw a second, larger circle as shown in Photo A. Drill holes slightly smaller than the branches every ¾ inch around the outer circle. Cut branches (these vary from 20 to 28 inches long) and use a crafts knife to whittle the base to fit the drilled holes. Place the vase in the center of the wood then insert the branches using wood glue to secure as shown in Photo B. Hot-glue faux butterflies to the branches.

CLEAN SLATE

Let your artistic side shine with painted rocks to dot your landscape. Use a small round-tip paintbrush and black acrylic paint to outline a simple design on a smooth rock. To make dots, dip the handle of the paintbrush into paint and dot onto the rock. Let the paint dry. Paint in the motifs using colorful acrylic paints and let dry. Spray with a matte all-weather clear coat; let dry.

FOR THE BIRDS

The sound of gently trickling water attracts birds to fly in for drinks and splashy baths. A lotus-like dripper attached to a submersible pump enhances a birdbath and creates a delightful garden accent. To make the birdbath, use a 6×48-inch PVC pipe as a base, anchoring 1 foot of it in the ground. Wrap the base with a length of twig fencing cut to fit as shown in the close-up photo, right. Set a 3-inch-deep saucer on the base. Place a few stones in the basin to secure the dripper and provide firm footing for birds. Always keep the pump covered with water.

ROCK-SOLID MAGNET

Give your fridge a beautiful lift. Print desired web images, such as those at *BHG.COM/diynature*, on a laser (not ink-jet) printer. For each magnet, dab a stone's flattest side with transfer medium, then place an image facedown on it. Starting at the image center, smooth out any creases and air bubbles with your finger. Remove excess medium with a damp cloth. Let dry at least 8 hours. Moisten the paper and let it sit for several minutes; then use a damp towel to rub away the paper and reveal the image. Seal with clear matte medium; let dry. Hot-glue a strong magnet, such as Rare Earth, to the back.

Fiesta Fever

Celebrate Cinco de Mayo with color-rich decorations that start the festivities exuberantly.

WOUND AROUND

Welcome guests to your home with a pretty wreath to celebrate Cinco de Mayo. Choose a spot on the wreath and start tightly wrapping yarn around the twig pieces. Continue wrapping until yarn covers a 4- to 5-inch section. Use small dabs of crafts glue to secure the ends of the yarn. Repeat with alternate yarn colors to achieve the desired look. This wreath uses six different colors of yarn, but you could use more or less.

STEP IN STYLE

Bold fabric, decoupage medium, and spray sealant make these concrete stones stand out and withstand the elements. When sealed, the fabric edges won't fray, and will be strong enough to hold up to both weather and foot traffic. A round print in bright hues, such as these suzani-style patterns, adds year-round color to the garden.

WHAT YOU NEED

crack-resistant concrete mix, such as Quikrete
round plastic pot liner
chicken wire, optional
outdoor fabric
decoupage medium
paintbrush
exterior-grade spray sealant

Tip: Make the stepping-stones about 1½ to 2 inches thick; thinner stones may crack. Lay the stones on smooth ground to prevent breakage. For added strength, place chicken wire in the middle of the concrete as you fill the mold.

WHAT YOU DO

1. Make a round concrete stepping-stone using a plastic pot liner—slightly larger than the print you've chosen—as a mold. Allow concrete to dry and cure according to manufacturer's instructions.

2. Cut fabric to desired-size circle. Cover the surface of the stepping-stone with decoupage medium as shown in Photo A. Place fabric on the coated concrete.

3. Cover the fabric with decoupage medium as shown in Photo B; let dry. Apply a second coat. When dry, spray the entire surface with sealant.

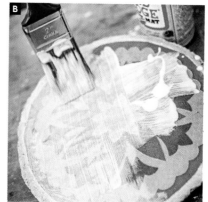

ALL-WEATHER BLOOMS

Make a big impact with bursts of colorful flowers to dot your party setting. Made just like the smaller accordion-folded tissue paper variety, these plate-size blooms are made with dollar-store plastic tablecloths. So even if it sprinkles, these pretty decorations won't wilt.

HEAVENLY HUES

Combine two or three shades of tablecloths to add interest to the flowers. To hang, tie a ribbon around the center.

Creative Containers

Pot your plants in unexpected containers you might find at home or in antiques stores or secondhand shops.

CARRIED AWAY

A cake carrier adds a touch of nostalgia to the garden. Poke a few holes in the bottom with an awl and line with rocks for drainage before planting.

ROLL WITH IT

Sure to bring smiles, roller skates make whimsical vases for fresh-cut blooms. Line each skate with a plastic cup or water bottle with the spout cut off. Fill the vessel halfway with water and arrange a bouquet in it. Carefully set the arrangement into the skate.

GREAT CRATE

Wonderfully portable, these pop crates hold oodles of plants yet can be easily moved with their built-in handles. To add legs, dollar-store rolling pins do the trick. Paint the pins with acrylic paint to match the crate—allowing some wood to show through for a shabby chic look—and let dry. Top-coat the legs with waterproof acrylic spray. Attach the legs to the crate using wood screws and glue. Before planting, line the crates with disposable metal baking pans to protect the wood.

A CUT ABOVE

Well-used bread boards grace the yard with character and offer a place to show off favorite cuttings. To attach a jar to a board, position the jar on the board and mark a pair of holes ½ inch in from edge of jar neck. Use heavy wire to secure jar to board through holes, twisting ends securely on the back of the board. Add clear epoxy for glass and wood for added stability where jar rests on board; let dry. Tie jute around the jar neck to camouflage the wire.

GRACEFUL GADGETS

Plentiful in secondhand shops and antiques stores, kitchen accessories from days gone by make darling landing spots for small plantings. Place a few small stones in the base for drainage and plant as usual. Group the gadgets for a fun themed display.

OLD-FASHIONED BEAUTY

Used indoors or out, sewing machine drawers make lovely planters. For a bigger impact, stack them by resting the top drawers on the sides of the drawers below. To protect the drawers, spray them with several coats of all-weather clear sealer and place potted plants in plastic cups before setting inside.

TOY TREASURE

While their play appeal may have faded, vintage metal toys make incredible finds for the garden. This doll high chair is just right to bring height to a planter that rests sturdily on the chair seat. Other toys that work magic in the garden include trikes, trucks, carriages, cradles, trains, and wagons.

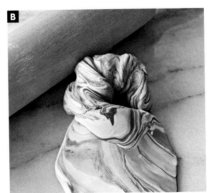

Custom Clay for Mom

Make Mother's Day extra special with gifts made of beautiful clay in all Mom's favorite colors.

WHAT A DISH

Swirls of colorful clay mimic the look of marble on this decorative dish. Knead four or five shades of polymer clay, then roll out ½-inch-diameter rods of each color. Lay the rods alongside each other, then twist together and fold the twisted rods in half as shown in Photo A. Twist and fold the clay again as shown in Photo B. Form the clay into a ball, then roll it out to ½-inch thickness. Lay a square dish on top and cut out the clay around the dish edges as shown in Photo C. Place the clay square inside an oven-safe glass bowl, allowing the corners to curve up slightly along the sides. Bake the clay in the bowl according to the clay manufacturer's instructions. Allow to cool, then remove the dish from the bowl. To smooth the corners of the dish, dampen and sand them slightly. Let dry.

HANG TIME

Cookie cutters make it easy to cut clay flowers for a mobile. Roll out desired shades of polymer clay to ¼-inch thickness, then use flower-shape cookie cutters to cut out the flowers as shown in Photo A. Press pieces of lace or other items onto the surface of each flower to create patterns; use a small straw to poke a hole for hanging in each flower as shown in Photo B. Place the shapes on a cookie sheet lined with parchment paper and bake according to the clay manufacturer's instructions. When cool, hang the shapes from a piece of driftwood using varying lengths of monofilament thread or fishing line. Tie a thick piece of jute or rope around the center of the driftwood and hang the mobile from a ceiling hook.

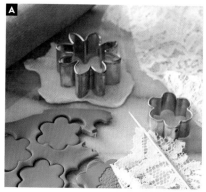

BUDDING IDEA

Inside this geometric clay vase is a glass test tube, which is just the right size for holding a few flower stems. Knead polymer clay to soften, then form it evenly around the test tube in a ball, making sure the tube is centered in the clay and the opening is uncovered. If needed, poke a pencil through the clay to clear the opening. Slice shallow pieces of clay off the ball using a sharp knife and straight strokes to create the geometric surface as shown in the close-up photo. Cut the base flat so test tube sits upright. Follow the manufacturer's instructions to bake the clay; let cool.

SAY CHEESE

Mom will love these custom clay cheese identifiers to show off at her next gathering. Roll out a thick, even layer of air-dry clay, then cut out shapes using small cookie cutters. Two shapes are needed for each marker, one plain and one stamped. Stamp letters and designs onto half the shapes as shown in Photo A. Cut 4-inch-long segments from the pointed ends of bamboo skewers. Sandwich a skewer segment between the clay layers as shown in Photo B. Seal the edges with a dampened finger; let dry. Wiggle the skewer periodically as the clay dries so it is removable and replaceable. Use a small brush to push brown acrylic paint into the stamped designs as shown in Photo C. Gently wipe paint from each surface with a clean cloth, allowing the designs to retain the paint; let dry.

Clear Winners

It's easy to create glossy, mesmerizing, see-through accessories using epoxy resin.

HERE COMES THE SUN

Hang these diamond suncatchers in a window and enjoy the shimmering effect.

Use an 8-inch-square silicone baking pan as the mold; then swirl in the color and embed objects such as large iridescent sequins, glitter, and metal findings. For the colorant, use those such as Castin' Craft Opaque Pigments and Transfer Dyes in blue opaque pigment and green transparent dye. Pop the hardened shape out of the mold. Hang it with a wire inserted through a hole drilled into the corner using a 1/16-inch bit. Refer to the basic instructions, below, for tips and safety instructions.

WHAT YOU NEED TO USE EPOXY RESIN
epoxy resin
hardener
two plastic measuring cups
stir sticks

HOW TO USE EPOXY RESIN
1. Gather supplies as shown in Photo A.
2. Working in a well-ventilated area, pour epoxy resin into a plastic measuring cup as shown in Photo B.
3. Add an equal amount of hardener on top of the epoxy resin in the same measuring cup as shown in Photo C.
4. Stir the mixture thoroughly for 2 minutes, scraping the sides occasionally and being careful to avoid air bubbles by not mixing too vigorously as shown in Photo D.
5. Pour the mixture into a clean, second measuring cup. Stir the mixture for 1 minute as shown in Photo E.
6. Pour the epoxy resin mixture into a mold, such as a silicone pan, a jewelry finding, or a bottle as shown in Photo F. If adding pigment or dye, partially fill mold with resin and mix in colorant using a toothpick before adding remainder of resin. (See page 60 for more information.) If adding objects to the resin, let it set up for a few minutes before putting in the object to keep it from sinking to the bottom of the mold. Allow to harden up to 72 hours to ensure a strong bond.

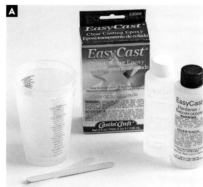

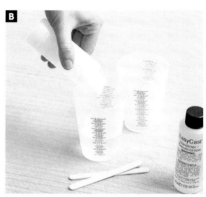

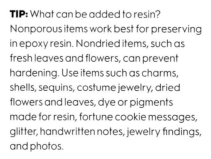

TIP: What can be added to resin? Nonporous items work best for preserving in epoxy resin. Nondried items, such as fresh leaves and flowers, can prevent hardening. Use items such as charms, shells, sequins, costume jewelry, dried flowers and leaves, dye or pigments made for resin, fortune cookie messages, glitter, handwritten notes, jewelry findings, and photos.

PENCHANT FOR PENDANTS

Bring a little formalwear to the holiday table. Blank jewelry pendants act as mini frames to show off your creativity. Paint the interior of the pendant, then fill the pendant with epoxy resin. Encapsulate an arrangement of charms, findings, and glitter into the liquid epoxy before it hardens. See page 58 for more information.

IT'S ONLY NATURAL

Bring a little piece of the outdoors to your desktop with paperweights that showcase natural materials. Use a flexible silicone muffin pan for the mold, add epoxy resin, then drop collected items into the resin and allow it to harden before popping it out of the mold. For more information, refer to the steps on page 58.

HOW TO ADD COLOR TO RESIN

1. Choose pigments and dyes made for epoxy resin.
2. Partially fill mold with epoxy resin. Pour a small amount of pigment or dye into wet resin as shown in Photo A.
3. Mix pigment or dye into resin with a crafts stick or toothpick as shown in Photo B. Fill mold with more resin.

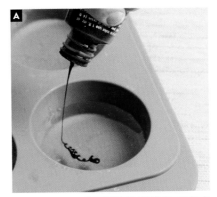

BOTTLED UP

Tiny wide-mouth glass bottles and vials become fascinating displays thanks to clear epoxy resin. Copper wire poked into the stoppers holds objects upright. For projects with a cork, decide whether it will be at the top or bottom. Cut a piece of wire the height of the bottle. Put a dot of crafts glue on one end and push it halfway into the bottom of the cork in the center; let dry. Choose an object to slide into the bottle. Glue it to the wire, trimming length first, if necessary, so the cork can be pushed snuggly back into the bottle after resin is added, and keeping in mind whether the cork will be at the top or bottom. If desired, add vellum details such as waves behind the ship by cutting the pieces, applying spray adhesive to the back, and carefully pressing inside the bottle; let dry. Add resin following the basic directions on page 58, leaving room for the object to be inserted without resin spilling over. If desired, sprinkle a small amount of coarse gold glitter into resin and use a toothpick to swirl it into the wet resin. Replace the cork on the bottle while plunging the object into the wet resin.

WINGING IT

Combine the beauty of a glittery insect-theme paperweight with a wire photo display. Bend a 5-inch-long wire into a paper-clip-style loop; set aside. Fill a silicone insect mold with resin and glitter. When hard, drill a ½-inch-deep hole into the paperweight, add glue to the straight end of the wire, and insert the wire into the hole.

OUT ON TOP

These bejeweled wine bottle stoppers make welcome hostess gifts and are easy to produce in multiples. Just fill a silicone gem mold with epoxy resin, stir in a drop of color, and drop in shimmery objects before the resin hardens. After the gems set up, pop them out of their molds and glue each one onto a cork.

PUT A RING ON IT

Identify wine glasses with charms that are so gorgeous they could double as jewelry. Create gems using small silicone molds, dots of colorant in resin, and glitter. Use a wire hoop found in jewelry-making section of a crafts store to attach each charm to a wine glass stem.

Easter Extraordinaire

SPRING HAS SPRUNG CENTERPIECE

A simple palette in tints of pink brings beauty and charm to the table. To make the centerpiece, fill a long metal tray with packing peanuts then drape preserved or fresh moss over it. Arrange flowers, candles, and eggs (glittered and solid) on the bed of green.

BUNNY PLACE CARDS

This cute bunny trail ushers Easter guests to their seats. Trace the bunny pattern on page 153; cut out. Place pattern facedown on the back of patterned cardstock and trace around it with a pencil. Cut out bunny silhouette along traced line. Make a pom-pom tail and attach to bunny using quick-setting gel glue.

GLITTERED EGGS

Add an element of glam to hard-boiled dyed eggs with a splash of gold glitter. Set the egg, narrow end down, into a bottle lid. Slightly dampen a sponge, dip it into decoupage medium or glue, then lightly apply it to the wide end of the egg; sprinkle with gold glitter. When dry, shake off excess glitter.

RISE AND SHINE

Combine flea market glass and ceramic dishes to form pretty pedestals for Easter desserts. Items such as candleholders, bowls, and vases configure shapely stands for plates and platters. Use strong glue for glass to adhere pieces together.

THINK PINK

Pink accents carry out the sweet spring theme. Use ribbon bows as curtain tiebacks, front door decor, and napkin ties.

**MAPLE SAGE
TURKEY**
Recipe on page 86

food

Treat holiday guests to a spectacular meal that will truly make the season special. Fabulous roasts, slow-cooker sides, and indulgent sweets create a memorable celebration.

CHOCOLATE TRUFFLE BROWNIES
Recipe on page 70

Brownie Points

Score some kisses from your sweetheart this Valentine's Day with a chocolatey treat that you baked yourself, especially for the occasion.

SWEET & SPICY
BROWNIE BITES

SWEET & SPICY BROWNIE BITES

WHAT YOU NEED

- 1¼ cups all-purpose flour
- 2 Tbsp. unsweetened cocoa powder
- 4 tsp. ground ancho chile pepper
- 1 tsp. ground cinnamon
- ½ tsp. kosher salt
- ½ tsp. freshly grated ginger
- 9 oz. quality dark chocolate (60% to 72% cacao), coarsely chopped
- 1 cup unsalted butter (2 sticks), cut into 1-inch pieces
- 1¼ cups granulated sugar
- ½ cup packed light brown sugar
- 5 eggs, room temperature
- 2 Tbsp. unsweetened cocoa powder (optional)
- ½ tsp. ground ancho chile pepper (optional)

WHAT YOU DO

1. Preheat oven to 350°F. Butter the sides and bottom of a 3-qt. square baking dish or a 13×9×2-inch baking pan; set aside.
2. In a medium bowl whisk together the flour, 2 Tbsp. cocoa powder, 4 tsp. chile pepper, cinnamon, salt, and ginger; set aside.
3. Place the chocolate and butter in the top of a double boiler or a large heatproof bowl. Set over a pan of barely simmering water (the bottom of the pan should not touch the water). Heat, stirring occasionally until the chocolate and butter are completely melted and combined. Remove from heat, keeping pan or bowl over water. Add both sugars; whisk until completely combined. Remove from water. Cool to room temperature.
4. Add three eggs to the chocolate mixture and whisk just until combined. Add the remaining eggs and whisk until combined. Do not overbeat the batter or brownies will be cakey.
5. Sprinkle the flour mixture over the chocolate mixture. Using a spatula (not a whisk), fold until there is just a trace amount of flour mixture visible.
6. Pour batter into the prepared dish or pan and smooth the top with a spatula. Bake 25 to 30 minutes or until a toothpick inserted near the center comes out with a few moist crumbs, rotating the pan halfway through baking. Cool completely on a wire rack. If desired, sprinkle with 2 Tbsp. cocoa

DEEP DARK CHOCOLATE BROWNIES

powder mixed with ½ tsp. ground ancho chile pepper. Makes 48 servings.

DEEP DARK CHOCOLATE BROWNIES

WHAT YOU NEED

- 1¼ cups all-purpose flour
- 2 Tbsp. unsweetened cocoa powder
- 1 tsp. kosher salt
- 11 oz. quality dark chocolate (60% to 72% cacao), coarsely chopped
- 1 cup unsalted butter, cut into 1-inch cubes
- 1 tsp. instant espresso coffee powder
- 1½ cups granulated sugar
- ½ cup packed light brown sugar
- 5 eggs, room temperature
- 2 tsp. vanilla
- 1 recipe Chocolate Ganache (optional)

WHAT YOU DO

1. Preheat oven to 350°F. Butter sides and bottom of a 3-qt. baking dish or 13×9×2-inch baking pan; set aside.
2. In a medium bowl whisk together flour, cocoa powder, and salt; set aside.
3. Place chocolate, butter, and espresso powder in a large heatproof bowl. Set over a pan of barely simmering water (bottom of bowl should not touch water). Heat, stirring occasionally, until chocolate and butter are melted and combined. Remove from heat, keeping bowl over water. Add sugars; whisk until completely combined. Remove bowl from water. Cool to room temperature.
4. Add three eggs to chocolate mixture; whisk just until combined. Add remaining eggs; whisk just until combined. Add vanilla; stir until combined.
5. Sprinkle flour mixture over chocolate mixture. Using a spatula (not a whisk), fold just until a trace amount of flour mixture is visible.
6. Pour batter into prepared dish; smooth top with a spatula. Bake 25 to 30 minutes or until a toothpick inserted near center comes out with a few moist crumbs, rotating pan halfway through baking. Cool on a wire rack. If desired, top with Chocolate Ganache. Makes 24 brownies.
Chocolate Ganache Place 6 oz. coarsely chopped dark chocolate in a heatproof bowl. Heat ½ cup heavy cream in a saucepan over medium heat just until bubbles form around edge; pour over chocolate. Let stand 1 minute. Whisk until smooth. Pour over cooled brownies. Spread evenly. Let stand 10 minutes. Refrigerate 15 minutes to set.

CHOCOLATE
TRUFFLE
BROWNIES

CHOCOLATE TRUFFLE BROWNIES

WHAT YOU NEED
Nonstick cooking spray
- ⅔ cup all-purpose flour
- ½ tsp. baking powder
- ½ tsp. salt
- ½ cup butter
- ½ cup milk or dark chocolate pieces
- 3 oz. unsweetened chocolate, chopped
- 1 cup sugar
- 1½ tsp. vanilla
- 3 eggs
- 1 4.63- to 5.25-oz. pkg. truffle-filled or plain milk or dark chocolate squares

WHAT YOU DO
1. Preheat oven to 325°F. Line a 9-inch square baking pan with foil, extending foil over edges. Coat foil with cooking spray. Stir together flour, baking powder, and salt.
2. In a medium saucepan over low heat stir butter, chocolate pieces, and unsweetened chocolate until melted. Cool slightly. Stir in sugar and vanilla. Add eggs, one at a time, beating with a spoon until combined. Stir in flour mixture just until combined. Spread batter in prepared pan. Bake 25 minutes.
3. Break chocolate squares into irregular-shape pieces. Sprinkle over warm brownies. Cool in pan on a wire rack. Using foil, lift brownies out of pan. Cut into bars. Makes 20 servings.

MALTED CHOCOLATE BROWNIES

WHAT YOU NEED
- 1¼ cups all-purpose flour
- 1 cup vanilla-flavor malted milk powder
- 1 Tbsp. unsweetened cocoa powder
- ½ tsp. kosher salt
- 10 oz. quality dark chocolate (60% to 72% cacao), coarsely chopped
- ¾ cup unsalted butter (1½ sticks) cut into 1-inch cubes
- 1 cup granulated sugar
- ½ cup packed brown sugar
- 5 eggs, room temperature
- 2 tsp. vanilla

WHAT YOU DO
1. Preheat oven to 350°F. Butter the sides and bottom of a 3-qt. rectangular baking dish or a 13×9×2-inch baking pan. Line the bottom with parchment, allowing edges to overhang the long sides of the pan by about 1 inch; butter the parchment.
2. In a medium bowl whisk together the flour, malted milk powder, cocoa powder, and salt.
3. Place the chocolate and butter in the top of a double boiler or a large heatproof bowl. Set over a pan of barely simmering water (the bottom of the pan should not touch the water). Heat, stirring occasionally, until the chocolate and butter are completely melted and combined. Remove from heat, keeping pan or bowl over water. Add both sugars; whisk until completely combined. Remove from water. Cool to room temperature.
4. Add three eggs to the chocolate mixture and whisk just until combined. Add the remaining eggs and whisk just until combined. Add the vanilla and stir until combined. Do not overbeat the batter or brownies will be cakey.
5. Sprinkle the flour mixture over the chocolate mixture. Using a spatula (not a whisk), fold until just a trace amount of flour is visible.
6. Pour batter into the prepared dish or pan; smooth the top with a spatula. Bake 25 to 30 minutes or until a toothpick inserted near the center comes out with a few moist crumbs, rotating the pan halfway through baking. Cool completely on a wire rack. Makes 24 servings.

RASPBERRY SWIRL BROWNIES

WHAT YOU NEED
- 1 cup fresh raspberries
- 1¼ cups all-purpose flour
- 2 Tbsp. unsweetened cocoa powder
- 1 tsp. kosher salt
- 11 oz. quality dark chocolate (60% to 72% cacao), coarsely chopped
- 1 cup unsalted butter (2 sticks), cut into 1-inch cubes
- 1 cup granulated sugar
- ½ cup packed light brown sugar
- 5 eggs, room temperature
- 1½ tsp. vanilla

WHAT YOU DO
1. Preheat oven to 350°F. Butter the sides and bottom of a 3-qt. rectangular baking dish or a 13×9×2-inch baking pan.
2. Place raspberries in a food processor; cover and blend until smooth. If desired, sieve puree to remove seeds. In a medium bowl whisk together the flour, cocoa powder, and salt.
3. Place the chocolate and butter in the top of a double boiler or a large heatproof bowl. Set over a pan of barely simmering water (the bottom of the pan should not touch the water). Heat, stirring occasionally, until the chocolate and butter are completely melted and combined. Remove from heat, keeping pan or bowl over water. Add both sugars; whisk until completely combined. Remove from water. Cool to room temperature.
4. Add three eggs to the chocolate mixture and whisk just until combined. Add the remaining eggs and whisk just until combined. Add the vanilla and stir until combined. Do not overbeat the batter or your brownies will be cakey.
5. Sprinkle the flour mixture over the chocolate mixture. Using a spatula (not a whisk), fold until just a trace amount of flour is visible.
6. Pour batter into the prepared pan; smooth the top with a spatula. Drizzle the raspberry puree over the batter and swirl in with a table knife or thin metal spatula. Bake the 25 to 30 minutes or until a toothpick inserted near the center comes out with a few moist crumbs, rotating the pan halfway through baking. Cool completely on a wire rack. Makes 24 servings.

RASPBERRY
SWIRL
BROWNIES

Quiche for Brunch

A savory filling in a rich, flaky, and buttery pastry crust makes an elegant main course.

SPINACH
PANCETTA
QUICHE

SPINACH PANCETTA QUICHE

WHAT YOU NEED

1   recipe Deep-Dish Pastry Shell (recipe, right)
8   oz. pancetta, chopped
2   large onions, thinly sliced (about 2 cups)
½   tsp. dried thyme, crushed
½   cup oil-packed dried tomatoes, drained and chopped
4   cups baby spinach
8   oz. Havarti cheese, shredded
6   eggs
2   cups plain fat-free Greek yogurt
1   cup milk
½   tsp. salt
¼   tsp. ground white pepper
⅛   tsp. ground nutmeg
    Fresh basil (optional)

WHAT YOU DO

1. Prepare Deep-Dish Pastry Shell. Preheat the oven to 325°F.

2. In a large skillet over medium heat cook the pancetta until lightly browned, about 10 to 12 minutes, stirring occasionally. With a slotted spoon, transfer pancetta to a paper-towel-lined plate, reserving 2 Tbsp. drippings in the skillet.

3. Return skillet to medium heat. Add the onions and dried thyme; cook, stirring occasionally, until tender and golden, 20 to 22 minutes. Stir in the dried tomatoes and cook 1 minute. Add the spinach and cook until wilted, 1 to 2 minutes. Remove from the heat and cool 10 minutes. Stir in pancetta and cheese.

4. For the custard, in a blender combine the eggs, yogurt, milk, salt, pepper, and nutmeg. Cover and blend until frothy.

5. Set the springform pan with the pastry shell on a baking sheet. Spoon onion mixture into the pastry shell. Pour in the custard. Bake 1 hour 20 minutes to 1 hour 30 minutes or until the top is lightly browned and the custard is just set in the center (165°F). Let cool in the pan 40 minutes. With a serrated knife, cut the pastry shell flush with the top of the pan. Carefully remove the springform pan ring. Cut the quiche into wedges. Makes 10 servings.

CHIPOTLE CHICKEN QUICHE

CHIPOTLE CHICKEN QUICHE

WHAT YOU NEED

1   recipe Deep-Dish Pastry Shell (recipe, right)
6   large eggs
2   cups plain fat-free Greek yogurt
1   cup milk
1   tsp. ground cumin
1   tsp. chili powder
½   tsp. ground chipotle chile pepper
½   tsp. salt
2   cups chopped cooked chicken (about 10 oz.)
1½ cups shredded cheddar cheese (6 oz.)
    Fresh salsa (optional)

WHAT YOU DO

1. Prepare Deep-Dish Pastry Shell; set aside on baking sheet. Preheat the oven to 325°F.

2. For the custard, in a blender combine the eggs, yogurt, milk, cumin, chili powder, ground chipotle, and salt. Cover and blend until frothy.

3. Place chicken and cheese in prebaked pastry shell. Pour custard over. Bake 1 hour 20 minutes to 1 hour 30 minutes or until the top is lightly browned and the custard is barely set in the center (165°F). Cool in the pan 40 minutes. With a serrated knife, cut the pastry shell flush with the top of the pan. Carefully remove the springform pan ring. Cut the quiche into wedges. If desired, top with fresh salsa. Makes 10 servings.

DEEP-DISH PASTRY SHELL

WHAT YOU NEED

2   cups all-purpose flour
1   tsp. salt
8   Tbsp. cold unsalted butter, cut into small pieces
1   large egg, lightly beaten
¼   cup cold water

WHAT YOU DO

1. In a food processor combine the flour and salt. Add the butter and pulse until the mixture resembles coarse crumbs. In a small bowl combine the egg and water; add to flour mixture and pulse just until the mixture just begins to clump together. Transfer dough onto a sheet of plastic wrap; fold the wrap over and press the crumbs until they hold together; shape into a disc. Wrap and chill at least 30 minutes.

2. Turn the dough out onto a lightly floured surface and roll it out to a 15-inch circle. Carefully roll the pastry around the rolling pin and transfer to a 9×2½-inch springform pan, pressing it into the sides. Trim the overhanging pastry to 1 inch and press it firmly against the outside of the ring to help prevent it from shrinking. Use the trimmings to fill any cracks. Freeze the shell 20 minutes.

3. Preheat the oven to 400°F. Place the springform pan on a baking sheet. Line the pastry shell with a double thickness of aluminum foil long enough to overhang the sides. Bake about 20 minutes or until the edge of the dough is lightly browned. Remove foil; bake 10 to 15 minutes longer or until lightly browned on the bottom. Transfer the baking sheet to a rack. Let the pastry cool. Makes 10 servings.

SWEET AND
SAVORY
GREENS
QUICHE

SWEET AND SAVORY GREENS QUICHE

WHAT YOU NEED
1   recipe Deep-Dish Pastry Shell (recipe, page 73)
2   Tbsp. extra-virgin olive oil
8   cups torn red Swiss chard (10 oz.)
1   medium red onion, chopped (1 cup)
3   cloves garlic, minced
¼   cup finely chopped golden raisins
3   Tbsp. pine nuts, toasted
2   tsp. balsamic vinegar
6   eggs
2   cups plain fat-free Greek yogurt
1   cup milk
½   tsp. salt
¼   tsp. ground white pepper
⅛   tsp. ground nutmeg
4   oz. provolone cheese, shredded (1 cup)
    Fresh herbs (optional)

WHAT YOU DO
1. Prepare Deep-Dish Pastry Shell; set aside on a baking sheet. Preheat oven to 325°F. Heat oil in an extra-large skillet over medium-high heat. Add the chard, onion, and garlic. Cook 4 to 6 minutes or just until chard is wilted. Add the raisins and pine nuts; cook until the raisins are plumped, about 2 minutes. Add the vinegar, tossing to combine. Remove from heat.

2. For custard, in a blender combine the eggs, yogurt, milk, salt, pepper, and nutmeg; cover and blend until frothy.
3. Place the chard mixture in the prebaked pastry shell. Sprinkle with cheese. Pour custard over. Bake 1 hour 20 minutes to 1 hour 30 minutes or until the top is lightly browned and the custard is just set (165°F) but still jiggles slightly in the center. Let stand 30 to 40 minutes. With a serrated knife, cut the pastry shell flush with the top of the pan. Carefully remove the springform pan ring. Cut the quiche into wedges. If desired, sprinkle with fresh herbs. Makes 10 servings.

CARAMELIZED PEAR AND BLUE CHEESE QUICHE

WHAT YOU NEED

- 1 recipe Deep-Dish Pastry Shell (recipe, page 73)
- 3 medium firm pears
- 2 Tbsp. unsalted butter
- 1 Tbsp. sugar
- ½ cup crumbled blue cheese
- 6 large eggs
- 2 cups plain fat-free greek yogurt
- 1 cup milk
- ½ tsp. salt
- ¼ tsp. ground white pepper
- ⅛ tsp. ground nutmeg
- Crumbled blue cheese
- Fresh sage leaves (optional)

WHAT YOU DO

1. Prepare Deep-Dish Pastry Shell; set aside on baking sheet. Preheat oven to 325°F.

2. Core and cut two of the pears into ½- to ¾-inch cubes. Thinly slice the remaining pear and reserve.

3. Melt 1 Tbsp. of the butter in a large skillet over medium-high heat. Add the cubed pears and sugar; cook, stirring occasionally, 7 to 8 minutes or until lightly browned. Transfer to the prebaked pastry shell and top with blue cheese. Melt the remaining 1 Tbsp. butter in the skillet; add the pear slices. Cook, stirring occasionally, 3 to 4 minutes or just until softened.

4. For the custard, in a blender combine the eggs, yogurt, milk, salt, pepper, and nutmeg. Blend until frothy.

5. Place the springform pan with the pastry shell on a baking sheet. Gently pour in the custard. Arrange the reserved pear slices in a spoke pattern on top of the quiche. Bake 1 hour 20 minutes to 1 hour 30 minutes or until the top is lightly browned and the custard is just set (165°F) but still jiggles slightly in the center. Let stand 30 to 40 minutes. With a serrated knife, cut the pastry shell flush with the top of the pan. Carefully remove the springform pan ring. Top with additional blue cheese and, if desired, sage leaves. Cut into wedges. Makes 10 servings.

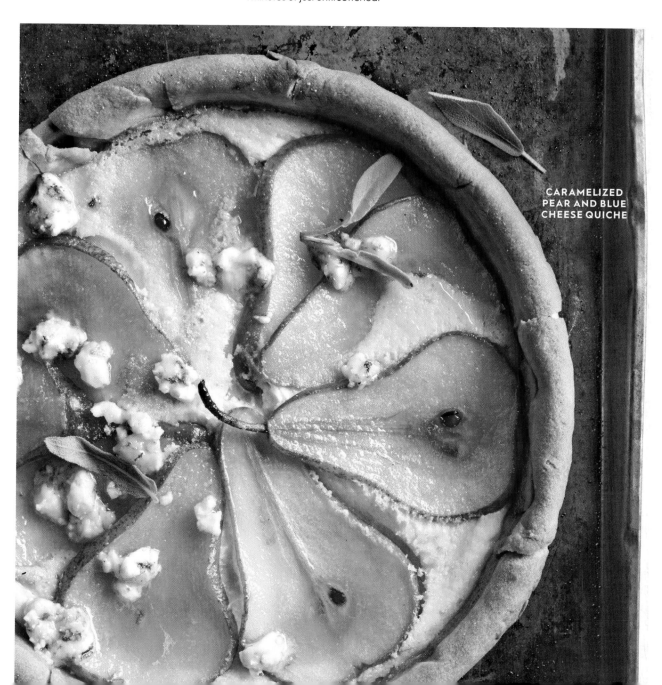

CARAMELIZED PEAR AND BLUE CHEESE QUICHE

Girls Night Outside

Invite your best girlfriends over for an al fresco spring or summer get-together that features fun, fresh, conversation-inspiring foods.

PIMIENTO
CHEESE

**BEET-DYED
DEVILED EGGS**

PIMIENTO CHEESE

WHAT YOU NEED

16 oz. aged sharp white cheddar
    cheese, shredded
1   8-oz. jar diced pimiento, drained
½   cup mayonnaise
2   Tbsp. shredded or finely chopped
    sweet onion
2   bottled mild or hot banana peppers,
    drained and finely chopped (2 Tbsp.)
    Pinch cayenne pepper
    Toasted baguette slices or crackers
    Red jalapeño jelly

WHAT YOU DO

1. In a large bowl stir together cheese,
pimiento, mayonnaise, onion, banana
peppers, and cayenne pepper. (For a
smoother consistency, beat mixture with
an electric mixer.) Transfer to a storage
container; cover and chill 4 hours or up
to 3 days. Serve on toast or crackers
with a small dollop of red jalapeño jelly.
Makes 28 servings.

BEET-DYED
DEVILED EGGS

WHAT YOU NEED

1   large beet (8 oz.)
2   cups water
1   cup white vinegar
12 hard-cooked eggs, peeled
⅓   cup mayonnaise
2   Tbsp. sweet pickle relish
1   Tbsp. whole grain mustard
    Salt

WHAT YOU DO

1. Wash, peel, and cube the beet. Place in a
medium saucepan with water and vinegar;
bring to boiling. Reduce heat and simmer,
covered, 15 minutes. Remove from heat;
cool completely (do not drain).
2. Place the eggs in the saucepan with
beet and liquid. Let stand 10 to 15 minutes.
Remove from liquid and slice in half
(discard beet and liquid). Remove the yolks
and set the whites aside.
3. Mash the yolks with the mayonnaise,
relish, mustard, and a pinch of salt. Pipe or
scoop filling into egg white halves. Sprinkle
with coarse salt. Makes 24 servings.

BEET-DYED DEVILED EGGS
Recipe on page 77

GRILLED FETA-BRINED CHICKEN
Recipe on page 80

GRILLED ROMAINE SALAD WITH PIQUILLO PEPPER DRESSING
Recipe on page 80

GARBANZO
BEAN AND
PARSLEY SALAD
Recipe on page 80

GRILLED ROMAINE SALAD WITH PIQUILLO PEPPER DRESSING

WHAT YOU NEED

1   12-oz. jar piquillo peppers or roasted red sweet peppers, drained (1⅓ cups)
1   cup sour cream
2   Tbsp. lemon juice
     Salt and black pepper
1   head romaine lettuce (about 1¼ lb.), quartered lengthwise
1   Tbsp. drained capers

WHAT YOU DO

1. For dressing, combine peppers, sour cream, and lemon juice in a blender. Cover and blend until smooth; season to taste with salt and pepper. Cover and chill until ready to serve or up to 1 week.
2. Place lettuce quarters on the rack of a covered grill directly over medium heat. Grill 1 to 3 minutes or until charred and slightly wilted, turning occasionally. Drizzle dressing over grilled romaine and top with capers. Makes 4 servings.

BOURBON STRAWBERRY SMASH

GARBANZO BEAN AND PARSLEY SALAD

WHAT YOU NEED

2   16-oz. cans garbanzo beans (chickpeas), rinsed and drained
2   tsp. olive oil
4   stalks celery, finely chopped (2 cups)
¼   of a sweet onion, finely chopped (¼ cup)
3   lemons, juiced (9 Tbsp.)
1   bunch Italian parsley, stems removed and leaves chopped (2 cups)
¼   cup olive oil
2   tsp. ground cumin
     Salt and black pepper
     Feta cheese, crumbled

WHAT YOU DO

1. In a large cast-iron skillet cook the beans over medium heat in 2 tsp. oil until crisp, about 15 minutes, stirring constantly. Set aside to cool.
2. In a medium bowl, soak the celery and chopped onion in lemon juice at room temperature for 30 minutes.
3. Add beans to the celery mixture. Fold in parsley. Add ¼ cup oil and cumin; toss to coat. Season to taste with salt and pepper. Serve or cover and chill up to 24 hours. Stir before serving. Sprinkle with feta cheese. Makes 6 servings.

GRILLED FETA-BRINED CHICKEN

WHAT YOU NEED

4   oz. feta cheese, crumbled
2   Tbsp. dried oregano
2½   tsp. kosher salt
2   tsp. cracked black pepper
4   cups water
2   to 3 lb. skinless, boneless chicken thighs
1   large lemon, halved
¼   cup olive oil
     Crumbled feta cheese
     Assorted fresh herbs (optional)

WHAT YOU DO

1. The day before serving, combine 4 oz. feta, oregano, salt, and cracked pepper, and water in a blender; cover and blend until smooth. Place chicken in an extra-large resealable plastic bag or container large enough to submerge chicken. Pour feta brine over chicken. Seal and chill at least 8 hours or overnight.
2. Remove chicken from brine and transfer to a paper-towel-lined tray. Discard brine. Pat chicken dry with paper towels and let rest at room temperature for 30 minutes.
3. Grill chicken on the rack of a covered grill directly over medium heat for 12 to 15 minutes or until done (at least 170°F), turning once.
4. Transfer chicken to a platter. Squeeze lemon halves over chicken and drizzle with oil. Season with additional salt and pepper. If desired, sprinkle with additional feta and herbs. Makes 6 servings.

BOURBON STRAWBERRY SMASH

WHAT YOU NEED

2   cups fresh strawberries, hulled and cut up
¼   cup simple syrup*
     Juice of 3 lemons (9 Tbsp.)
¼   cup fresh mint leaves
18   oz. (2¼ cups) bourbon
2   cups club soda, chilled
     Crushed ice

WHAT YOU DO

1. In a 2-qt. glass pitcher, using a muddler or a wooden spoon, mash strawberries, syrup, lemon juice, and mint leaves together. Add bourbon and club soda. Stir in ice to fill pitcher. Garnish each drink with additional mint sprigs. Makes 6 servings.
*Simple Syrup: In a small saucepan heat and stir ⅓ cup sugar and ⅓ cup water until sugar is dissolved. Remove from heat and cool. Cover and chill up to 2 weeks. Makes ½ cup.

LEMON MERINGUE TARTS

WHAT YOU NEED

1⅓ cups all-purpose flour
⅓   cup granulated sugar
2   tsp. finely shredded lemon zest
½   cup cold butter (no substitutes)
2   egg yolks, beaten
2   Tbsp. cold water
1   egg yolk
½   cup sweetened condensed milk
¼   cup lemon juice
⅛   tsp. salt
½   cup granulated sugar
2   tsp. cornstarch
1   tsp. finely shredded lemon zest
⅓   cup lemon juice

LEMON MERINGUE TARTS

3   Tbsp. water
2   Tbsp. butter
3   egg yolks
4   egg whites
1   tsp. vanilla
½   tsp. cream of tartar
½   cup granulated sugar
1   Tbsp. powdered sugar
    Honey (optional)

WHAT YOU DO

1. For tart shells, in a large bowl stir together flour, the ⅓ cup sugar, and 2 tsp. lemon zest. Using a pastry blender, cut in the ½ cup cold butter until mixture is crumbly. Add 2 egg yolks and 2 Tbsp. water to flour mixture; stir with a fork to combine. Gently knead the dough just until a ball forms. If necessary, cover with plastic wrap; chill 30 to 60 minutes or until dough is easy to handle.

2. Preheat oven to 375°F. Divide chilled dough into 12 pieces. Press each piece onto bottom and halfway up the sides of a 3-inch muffin cup. Bake 10 minutes or until golden. Cool in muffin cups 10 minutes. Remove and arrange in a 15×10×1-inch baking pan. Reduce the oven temperature to 350°F.

3. For lemon filling, in a small bowl whisk together the egg yolk, milk, lemon juice, and salt.

4. For lemon curd, in a small saucepan stir together the ½ cup sugar and the cornstarch. Stir in 1 tsp. lemon zest, the ⅓ cup lemon juice, 3 Tbsp. water, and 2 Tbsp. butter. Cook and stir over medium heat until thickened and bubbly. Remove from heat.

5. Stir about half the mixture into the 3 egg yolks. Return all mixture to saucepan. Return to heat. Cook and stir 2 minutes more. Cover to keep warm.

6. For meringue, in a medium bowl beat egg whites, vanilla, and cream of tartar with mixer on medium until soft peaks form. Gradually add ½ cup sugar, beating on high until stiff peaks form.

7. To assemble, spoon about 1 Tbsp. lemon filling into each baked crust; top with 1 Tbsp. lemon curd. Top each generously with meringue, spreading to edges of crusts. Sift powdered sugar over tarts. Bake 12 minutes or until golden. Cool in pan on a wire rack. Cover loosely with foil and chill within 1 hour. If desired, drizzle the chilled tarts with honey before serving. Makes 12 servings.

Sunday Supper Pot Roast

A pot roast bubbling away in the oven—and the enticing aroma it gives off—is the epitome of comfort. Gather friends or family on a fall weekend to start the week right.

TOMATO-HERB POT ROAST

TOMATO-HERB POT ROAST

WHAT YOU NEED

3	to 3½ lb. boneless beef chuck pot roast
½	tsp. salt
¼	tsp. black pepper
2	Tbsp. olive oil
1	cup finely chopped onion
4	cloves garlic, minced
1	15-oz. can tomato sauce
1	Tbsp. tomato paste
½	cup dry red wine or beef broth
¼	cup snipped fresh Italian parsley
¼	cup pitted, quartered Kalamata olives
2	anchovy fillets, patted dry and finely chopped
2	15- to 16-oz. cans cannellini beans (white kidney beans), rinsed and drained
	Cracked black pepper
2	Tbsp. finely shredded Parmesan cheese
	Snipped fresh Italian parsley

WHAT YOU DO

1. Preheat oven to 325°F. Trim fat from meat. Season meat with salt and pepper. In a 6-qt. Dutch oven brown roast on all sides in 1 Tbsp. hot oil over medium-high heat. Transfer to a plate.

2. Add onion and three cloves garlic to Dutch oven. Cook and stir 3 minutes. Stir in tomato sauce, tomato paste, wine, the ¼ cup parsley, olives, and anchovy fillets. Return roast to Dutch oven. Bring to boiling. Transfer to oven. Roast, covered, 2½ hours or until meat is tender.

3. Transfer meat to a platter; cover to keep warm. Bring liquid in Dutch oven to boiling. Reduce heat. Simmer, uncovered, 10 to 15 minutes or until slightly thickened.

4. Meanwhile, heat the remaining 1 Tbsp. oil in a large skillet over medium-high heat. Add the remaining clove garlic. Cook and stir 30 seconds. Add beans; cook and stir 2 to 3 minutes or until heated through.

GARLIC-BACON
POT ROAST

5. Transfer beans to platter with beef. Sprinkle with cracked pepper, Parmesan cheese, and additional parsley. Serve with sauce. Makes 8 servings.

GARLIC-BACON POT ROAST

WHAT YOU NEED
3 to 3½ lb. beef chuck pot roast
½ tsp. kosher salt
¼ tsp. freshly cracked black pepper
2 Tbsp. olive oil
6 slices applewood smoked bacon, diced
1½ cups coarsely chopped onion
8 cloves garlic, smashed
1 14.5-oz. can reduced-sodium beef broth
2 Tbsp. snipped fresh thyme
1 Tbsp. snipped fresh rosemary
3 medium carrots, cut into 2-inch pieces
10 small red and/or yellow new potatoes, quartered
 Fresh thyme sprigs

WHAT YOU DO
1. Preheat oven to 325°F. Trim fat from meat; season with salt and pepper. In a 6-qt. Dutch oven brown roast on all sides in hot oil over medium-high heat. Transfer to a plate.

2. Add bacon to oil in Dutch oven. Cook until browned, stirring occasionally. Transfer half of the cooked bacon to a paper-towel-lined plate; cover and chill until serving. Add onion and garlic to Dutch oven. Cook and stir about 5 minutes or until onion is tender and starting to brown. Return roast to Dutch oven. Add broth, the 2 Tbsp. thyme, and the rosemary. Bring to boiling. Cover; transfer to oven. Roast 1¾ hours. Add carrots and potatoes. Roast, covered, 45 minutes more or until meat and vegetables are tender.

3. Transfer meat and vegetables to a platter; cover to keep warm. Skim fat from liquid; strain liquid through a fine-mesh sieve into a bowl. Return strained liquid to Dutch oven. Bring to boiling; reduce heat. Simmer, uncovered, 10 to 15 minutes or until slightly thickened. Serve sauce with meat and vegetables. Sprinkle with reserved bacon and thyme sprigs. Makes 8 servings.

COFFEE-BRAISED
POT ROAST

3. Roast, covered, 1¾ hours. Add potatoes. Roast, covered, 45 minutes to 1 hour more or until meat and vegetables are tender.
4. Transfer meat and vegetables to a platter; cover to keep warm. Bring liquid in Dutch oven to boiling. Reduce heat. Simmer, uncovered, 10 to 15 minutes or until slightly thickened. Serve sauce with meat and potatoes. If desired, sprinkle with additional crushed red pepper. Makes 8 servings.

SOY-GINGER POT ROAST

WHAT YOU NEED
3 to 3½ lb. beef chuck pot roast
½ tsp. kosher salt
¼ tsp. black pepper
2 Tbsp. olive oil
1½ cups coarsely chopped onion
3 cloves garlic, minced
2 Tbsp. grated fresh ginger
16 oz. button mushrooms
1 14.5-oz. can reduced-sodium beef broth
¼ cup soy sauce
¼ cup snipped fresh cilantro
2 red sweet peppers, cut into 2-inch pieces
   Snipped fresh cilantro
   Hot cooked egg noodles

WHAT YOU DO
1. Preheat oven to 325°F. Trim fat from meat; season with salt and black pepper. In a large Dutch oven brown roast on all sides in hot oil over medium-high heat. Transfer to a plate.
2. Add onion, garlic, and ginger to Dutch oven. Cook and stir 5 minutes or until onion is softened. Add mushrooms, broth, soy sauce, and the ¼ cup cilantro. Return roast to Dutch oven. Bring to boiling. Cover; transfer to oven. Roast 2 hours. Add sweet peppers. Cover; roast 30 minutes more or until meat and vegetables are tender.
3. Transfer meat and vegetables to a platter; cover to keep warm. Bring liquid in Dutch oven to boiling; reduce heat. Simmer, uncovered, 10 to 15 minutes or until slightly thickened. Serve sauce with meat and vegetables. Sprinkle with additional cilantro. Serve with cooked noodles. Makes 8 servings.

COFFEE-BRAISED POT ROAST

WHAT YOU NEED
3 to 3½ lb. beef chuck pot roast
1 tsp. salt
½ tsp. black pepper
1 Tbsp. vegetable oil
1 large onion, halved and sliced
1 green sweet pepper, cut into 2-inch pieces
3 cloves garlic, minced
¾ cup beef broth
1 8-oz. can crushed pineapple (juice pack)
1 Tbsp. instant espresso or French roast coffee powder
¼ tsp. crushed red pepper
¼ tsp. ground allspice
2 lb. sweet potatoes, peeled, halved lengthwise, and cut into 2-inch pieces
   Crushed red pepper (optional)

WHAT YOU DO
1. Preheat oven to 325°F. Trim fat from meat. Rub meat with salt and black pepper. In a 6-qt. Dutch oven brown roast on all sides in hot oil over medium-high heat. Transfer to a plate.
2. Add onion, sweet pepper, and garlic to Dutch oven. Cook and stir 4 to 5 minutes or until onion and garlic are tender and starting to brown. Return roast to Dutch oven. Add broth, pineapple, espresso powder, the ¼ tsp. crushed red pepper, and allspice. Bring to boiling.

SOY-GINGER
POT ROAST

Early Bird Thanksgiving

Coordinating the preparation of the many dishes of this holiday celebration is perhaps the biggest feat of the feast. These make-ahead recipes will keep you in control.

GARLIC ROSEMARY DRESSING
Recipe on page 88

CREAM CHEESE MASHERS WITH KALE PESTO
Recipe on page 90

MAPLE SAGE TURKEY

MAPLE SAGE TURKEY

This turkey gets a double dose of maple with sugar in the dry brine and syrup in the glaze for a smoky, juicy slice. Dry brine is easier to manage than wet brine—no salty water slopping around. The salt and sugar rub is sprinkled on the turkey a few days ahead of time, working the bird into a juicy and tender state (Bonus: The turkey can finish thawing while the dry brine does its work). Once the bird is dry-brined, no more work until roasting. Slip it straight into the oven and finish it with the glaze.

WHAT YOU NEED
1   14-lb. frozen turkey
3   Tbsp. coarse kosher salt
3   Tbsp. maple sugar or packed brown sugar
1   tsp. dried sage, crushed
½   tsp. freshly ground black pepper
2   cups hot water
½   cup maple syrup
¼   cup unsalted butter
4   tsp. finely shredded orange zest

1   tsp. ground chipotle chile pepper
1   tsp. whole black peppercorns

WHAT YOU DO
1. Partially thaw turkey in the refrigerator 1 to 2 days or until breast meat gives when pressed; it is fine if the turkey is still somewhat frozen. Remove turkey from packaging; pat dry.
2. For rub, in a small bowl mix salt, sugar, dried sage, and black pepper. Rub evenly over turkey. Place turkey, breast side up, on a rack in a large roasting pan. Cover loosely with plastic wrap. Refrigerate 3 days or until fully thawed. Remove plastic wrap the night before cooking.
3. Preheat oven to 450°F. Remove neck and giblets from turkey cavity. Loop kitchen string around drumsticks; tie securely to tail. Pour 2 cups hot water into roasting pan with turkey. Turn heat down to 350°F. Roast turkey, uncovered, 2 hours. (If breast browns too quickly, cover loosely with foil.)
4. For glaze, in a small saucepan heat maple syrup, butter, orange zest, chipotle,

and peppercorns until warm. After 2 hours of roasting, generously brush turkey with maple glaze every 20 minutes for 40 to 60 minutes or until meat thermometer inserted in the thigh (not touching bone) registers at least 175°F. Remove turkey from oven. Tent loosely with foil; let stand 15 minutes. Reserve drippings for gravy. Makes 18 servings.

EARLY BIRD TURKEY GRAVY

Gravy is the last-minute stress note on Thanksgiving: Is there enough? Can I finish it in time? Ditch the stress by making gravy and stashing it in the freezer.

WHAT YOU NEED
6   stalks celery, cut up
4   carrots, unpeeled and cut up
2   onions, unpeeled and quartered
2   Tbsp. unsalted butter, melted
5   lb. bone-in, skin-on turkey thighs or drumsticks
½   cup dry white wine

8   cups water
1   Tbsp. whole black peppercorns
2   bay leaves
½   cup unsalted butter
½   cup all-purpose flour
¼   cup cornstarch
¼   cup cold water
1   cup turkey drippings (optional)
    Marjoram leaves

WHAT YOU DO

1. For turkey broth, preheat oven to 400°F. Place celery, carrots, and onions in a roasting pan; add 2 Tbsp. melted butter and toss to coat. Top vegetables with turkey. Roast turkey pieces and vegetables, uncovered, 1 hour. Transfer turkey and vegetables to an 8-qt. pot. Stir wine into hot roasting pan; scrape up browned bits. Add to pot with turkey and vegetables. Add 8 cups water to the pot; add peppercorns and bay leaves. Bring water to boiling; reduce heat and simmer, covered, 1 hour. Use a slotted spoon to remove turkey and vegetables from broth.* Strain broth through a fine-mesh sieve, discard solids and bay leaves. Measure 6 cups broth. Cover and chill any remaining broth for another use.

2. In a 4-qt. pot melt ½ cup butter over medium heat. When it foams up, add the flour and whisk until smooth. Reduce heat to medium-low and cook 10 minutes, stirring frequently, until it darkens to deep caramel color. Remove from heat. Carefully stir in broth (mixture may spatter). Cool gravy; transfer to freezer containers. Seal, label, and freeze up to 1 month.

3. Thaw gravy overnight in refrigerator. Reheat in a large saucepan over medium heat, stirring occasionally. In a small bowl stir together the cornstarch and cold water. Add to gravy. Cook and stir until thickened and bubbly. Cook and stir 2 minutes more. If desired, add 1 cup turkey drippings from freshly cooked turkey. Season to taste with salt and black pepper. Stir in marjoram leaves before serving. Makes 24 servings.

*Remove turkey from bones; reserve for another use.

LEMON ROSEMARY POTATO ROLLS

These will be a family favorite; instant potato flakes add tenderness to these rolls, and lemon and rosemary make them extra-special.

WHAT YOU NEED

2   Tbsp. instant mashed potato flakes
2   cups boiling water
¾   cup unsalted butter, cubed
⅓   cup sugar
2   Tbsp. finely chopped fresh rosemary leaves
1   Tbsp. finely shredded lemon zest
2   tsp. salt
2   packages active dry yeast (1½ Tbsp.)
4   large eggs
8   cups all-purpose flour
1   Tbsp. heavy cream, half-and-half, or light cream
    Herbed Lemon Butter (optional)

WHAT YOU DO

1. In a large mixing bowl combine potato flakes and boiling water. Mix in butter, sugar, rosemary, lemon zest, and salt. Let stand 10 minutes.

2. In small bowl sprinkle yeast over ¼ cup warm water (105°F to 115°F); stir to dissolve yeast. Set aside 5 minutes until foamy.

3. Whisk eggs into butter mixture, then the yeast mixture. Stir in flour, 2 cups at a time, until a thick, sticky dough forms.

4. Turn dough out onto a floured surface; quickly pat dough into a 12×16 rectangle. Use a floured knife to cut dough into 48 pieces. With floured hands, pull pieces into balls. Arrange side by side in 2 lightly greased 13×9-inch pans or disposable foil pans. Cover with plastic wrap; refrigerate 2 hours or up to 3 days. Or cover with plastic wrap, then foil; freeze up to 1 month.

5. To bake, let dough rise at room temperature 1 hour (about 2 hours for frozen dough) or until doubled. Preheat oven to 375°F. Brush roll tops with cream. Bake 20 to 25 minutes or until browned. Serve warm with Herbed Lemon Butter (if using). Makes 48 servings.

Herbed Lemon Butter: Let 1 stick (½ cup) butter stand at room temperature for 10 minutes. In a shallow dish combine 1 Tbsp. finely shredded lemon zest and 1 Tbsp. snipped fresh rosemary. Gently roll butter in lemon peel mixture to coat. Wrap in plastic wrap. Cover and chill up to 1 week. Slice and serve with rolls.

SAVORY COLLARD
GREENS

CARAMELIZED VEGGIE
LENTIL SALAD

SAVORY COLLARD GREENS

Collard greens have a meaty heartiness that makes them more satisfying than many other greens.

WHAT YOU NEED

5 lb. collard greens (about 6 bunches), cleaned
½ lb. pancetta, cut into ½-inch pieces
12 cloves garlic (1 bulb), coarsely chopped
½ tsp. crushed red pepper
2 cups chicken broth
¼ cup balsamic vinegar
    Salt and black pepper
    Crushed red pepper (optional)

WHAT YOU DO

1. Fold each collard green leaf in half; slice away the tough center stem. Stack the leaves, roll tightly, and slice into ½-inch ribbons (about 40 cups). Transfer to a resealable plastic bag and refrigerate up to 3 days.
2. In a 6- to 8-qt. pot cook pancetta over medium heat for 8 minutes or until crisp and browned. Transfer with a slotted spoon to paper towels; set aside. Add garlic and ½ tsp. crushed red pepper to drippings in pot; cook 2 minutes.
3. Add about half the sliced collard greens to pot. Pour in chicken broth and vinegar. Cover and cook 5 minutes to allow the collards to cook down. Add remaining collard greens. Cover and bring to boiling. Reduce heat and simmer on low for 20 to 30 minutes or until greens are tender, stirring occasionally. Season to taste with salt and black pepper. Top with cooked pancetta and, if desired, additional crushed red pepper. Makes 8 servings.

CARAMELIZED VEGGIE LENTIL SALAD

WHAT YOU NEED

2½ lb. fennel bulbs, trimmed, cored, quartered, and thinly sliced (if desired, reserve fronds)
1 lb. carrots (about 6), peeled and finely chopped
3 Tbsp. unsalted butter, melted
    Salt and pepper
2 cups dried French green lentils
6 cloves garlic, minced
2 bay leaves

4 cups reduced-sodium chicken broth
½ cup extra-virgin olive oil
3 Tbsp. country Dijon-style mustard
1 Tbsp. balsamic vinegar
1 Tbsp. honey
2 cups loosely packed Italian parsley leaves, finely chopped
2 large shallots, finely chopped (⅓ cup)
6 large leaves sage, finely chopped (¼ cup)

WHAT YOU DO

1. Preheat oven to 425°F. In a 15×10×1-inch baking pan toss fennel and carrots with melted butter; season generously with salt and pepper. Roast, uncovered, about 30 minutes, or until tender and caramelized, stirring once or twice.
2. Meanwhile, wash and rinse the lentils. In a 4-qt. pot combine lentils, garlic, bay leaves, and chicken broth; bring to boiling. Reduce heat and simmer, uncovered, 20 to 25 minutes or until tender. Drain any remaining liquid from lentils. Remove and discard bay leaves. Stir in ½ tsp. salt.
3. In an extra-large bowl whisk together the olive oil, mustard, balsamic vinegar, and honey. Stir in lentil mixture, parsley, shallots, and sage; stir in caramelized vegetables.
4. Cover and refrigerate up to 2 days. Serve cold or at room temperature. If desired, garnish with additional parsley and fennel fronds. Makes 21 (½ cup) servings.

GARLIC ROSEMARY DRESSING

This generous batch of simple rustic dressing is livened up with garlic and herbs and two different breads for an interesting texture.

WHAT YOU NEED

1 18-oz. loaf rustic white bread, cut into 1-inch cubes (about 10 cups)
1 18-oz. loaf rustic whole wheat bread, cut into 1-inch cubes (about 10 cups)
½ cup unsalted butter
2 lb. yellow onions, chopped (6½ cups)
6 stalks celery, chopped (3 cups)
2 tsp. celery seeds
10 cloves garlic, minced
4 large eggs, beaten
3 Tbsp. finely chopped rosemary leaves

2　Tbsp. finely chopped sage leaves
3　to 4 cups turkey or chicken stock
2½　tsp. salt
1　tsp. freshly ground black pepper
¼　cup olive oil
2　cups fresh or frozen cranberries

WHAT YOU DO

1. Preheat oven to 350°F. Spread bread cubes in two shallow baking pans. Toast 15 minutes or until lightly golden, stirring frequently. Cool.

2. In a large skillet, heat butter over medium-high heat. Add onions, celery, and celery seeds. Cook and stir until soft, about 10 minutes.

3. In an extra-large bowl combine garlic, eggs, rosemary, and sage. Add 3 cups of the stock, salt, and pepper. Working in batches, add toasted bread cubes and cooked onion mixture; gently toss to combine.

4. Divide dressing between two lightly greased 3-qt. baking dishes. Drizzle each dish with 2 Tbsp. olive oil. Cover dishes with foil; refrigerate overnight.

5. Preheat oven to 350°F. Bake dressing, covered, 25 minutes. Remove foil; increase oven temperature to 375°F. Bake about 20 minutes more or until tops are lightly browned and dressing is heated through. Stir 1 cup cranberries into each dish. Let stand 10 minutes before serving. Makes 12 servings.

SWEET POTATO-CAULIFLOWER FRITTERS

The comfort food highlight of the meal are crispy, creamy sweet potato patties. Cauliflower adds heartiness to the potato's sweetness; together they make deliciously savory fritters.

WHAT YOU NEED

2　lb. sweet potatoes (about 5 medium), unpeeled, scrubbed, ends trimmed, and cut into 1½- to 2-inch chunks
1　small head cauliflower (2 lb.), cored and broken into 1½- to 2-inch florets
2　Tbsp. olive oil
　　Salt and Pepper
1　medium red onion (1 cup), peeled and cut into chunks
2　cloves garlic, smashed and peeled
2　tsp. finely chopped sage
2　tsp. finely chopped rosemary
¼　tsp. cayenne pepper

SWEET POTATO-CAULIFLOWER FRITTERS

1　egg
¾　cup all-purpose flour
　　Vegetable, coconut, or safflower oil
1½　cups panko bread crumbs

WHAT YOU DO

1. Preheat oven to 400°F. Place sweet potatoes and cauliflower in separate shallow baking pans. Drizzle with the olive oil and season generously with salt and pepper. Roast, uncovered, 30 minutes or just until browned and tender, stirring halfway through. Let stand 10 minutes.

2. In a food processor combine onion and garlic; pulse until finely chopped. Transfer to an extra-large bowl. Add cauliflower to processor and pulse until chopped; transfer to the bowl with onion. Process sweet potatoes, half at a time until coarsely mashed. Add to bowl with cauliflower.

3. Add sage, rosemary, 1½ tsp. salt, ½ tsp. black pepper, and cayenne pepper to

potato mixture. Stir to combine. Add egg and flour; stir to combine. Cover and refrigerate potato mixture 2 hours or up to 2 days.

4. In a large skillet heat 1 inch of oil over medium heat for 10 minutes or until 350°F. Place panko in a shallow dish. Using a ⅓-cup measure, shape the sweet potato mixture into 16 balls and roll in panko to coat. Add to hot oil in skillet, five or six at a time. Cook 6 to 8 minutes or until browned and heated through (160°F), turning to brown evenly. Transfer to a paper-towel-lined tray to drain. Serve warm. Makes 16 servings.

CREAM CHEESE MASHERS WITH KALE PESTO

WHAT YOU NEED

- 5 lb. russet potatoes, peeled and cut into large pieces
- 4 cloves garlic, peeled and smashed
- 1 Tbsp. kosher salt
- 1 cup heavy cream, half-and-half, or light cream
- ¾ cup unsalted butter
- 12 oz. cream cheese, softened and cut into small pieces
  Black pepper
- 6 cups chopped kale leaves and stems (¾ of a large bunch; 6 oz.)
- ¾ cup olive oil
- 6 cloves garlic, peeled
- ¾ cup grated Parmesan cheese
- ⅓ cup dry-roasted, salted sunflower kernels
- 6 Tbsp. lemon juice
  Kosher salt
  Water

WHAT YOU DO

1. Place potatoes and garlic in a 6-qt. pot and add water to cover; stir in salt. Bring to boiling. Reduce heat; simmer, covered, 20 minutes or until very tender. Drain. Return potatoes to pot.

2. While potatoes are cooking, melt butter in a small saucepan; add cream. Keep warm over low heat.

3. Mash potatoes in the cooking pot with a potato masher. Stir in the cream cheese. Slowly add the butter mixture, stirring it in to melt the cream cheese. The potatoes may look soupy at first, but they will quickly absorb the liquid. Season to taste with salt and pepper. Keep mashed potatoes warm in slow cooker set on low up to 4 hours. Top with kale pesto.

4. For Kale Pesto, place chopped kale leaves and stems, olive oil, garlic, Parmesan, and sunflower kernels in a food processor. Cover and process until a smooth paste forms. Blend in lemon juice and salt to taste. If desired, thin with water. Serve Kale Pesto on Cream Cheese Mashers. Makes 22 servings.

Tip: Mashed potatoes can be made 4 hours before dinner and kept warm in a 6-qt. slow cooker on low heat. Stir before serving. Kale pesto can be made up to 1 month ahead and frozen in a resealable plastic freezer bag. Thaw overnight and serve at room temperature.

MAPLE PANNA COTTA

WHAT YOU NEED

- 2 cups maple syrup
- 6 cups half-and-half or light cream
- 4 tsp. unflavored gelatin
- 1 tsp. pure vanilla
- ½ tsp. salt
- 2 cups heavy cream
- ¼ cup maple or granulated sugar
  Fresh currants (optional)

WHAT YOU DO

1. In a 3-qt. saucepan bring maple syrup to boiling. Reduce heat. Simmer, uncovered, 15 minutes. Whisk in half-and-half.

2. Remove from heat. Sprinkle gelatin over cream mixture. Let stand for 5 minutes or until gelatin is wrinkled and soft.

3. Warm gently over low heat, whisking until gelatin is dissolved (do not simmer or bring to a boil). Whisk in vanilla and salt.

4. Divide panna cotta among twelve 6-oz. glasses or bowls. Cover with plastic wrap. Refrigerate 2 hours until set or up to 3 days.

5. In a large bowl beat cream and maple sugar with a mixer until cream holds soft peaks. To serve, top each serving with whipped cream and, if desired, garnish with currants. Makes 12 servings.

MAPLE PANNA COTTA

Cake & Ice Cream Cupcakes

Sure, cake and ice cream are a terrific pair. Now, how about ice cream tucked into cake?

CAKE & ICE CREAM CUPCAKES

When you start with bakery cupcakes, it so easy to add flavor and fun.

WHAT YOU NEED

12 bakery cupcakes
1   quart ice cream
    Toppings

WHAT YOU DO

To make the ice cream rounds, remove brick-style ice cream from the carton. Working quickly, cut the ice cream block into slices. Use a round cookie cutter to cut out circles. Store in the freezer until ready to use. Place the leftover ice cream in a container and refreeze for another time. When it's time to assemble the cupcakes, split them in half and simply layer on the ingredients as shown in the lists below. Serve immediately!

GRASSHOPPER
- Frosted chocolate cupcake
- Mint chocolate chip ice cream
- Chocolate syrup
- Chocolate-mint candies, chopped

SALTED CARAMEL
- Frosted white cupcake
- Salted caramel ice cream
- Caramel ice cream topping
- Flaked sea salt

BIRTHDAY
- Yellow Cupcake
- Strawberry frosting
- Strawberry ice cream
- Confetti ice cream · White frosting
- Sprinkles · Cherry

NEAPOLITAN MASH-UP
- Chocolate-frosted white cupcake
- Neapolitan ice cream
- Strawberry jam

CHIP, CHIP HOORAY
- Frosted chocolate cupcake
- Cookie dough ice cream
- Chocolate syrup · Chocolate chips

A LITTLE NUTTY
- Frosted white cupcake
- Butter pecan ice cream
- Caramel ice cream topping
- Toasted pecans

summer

SOAK UP THE SUNNY SEASON
Holidays, get-togethers, outdoor retreats—there's so much to enjoy in the summer. Make the most of it with grand party ideas and welcoming projects.

Fun in the Sun

Make the most of a cloudless day. Lay summery images on light-sensitive surfaces and watch as solar rays work their magic.

JUST BEACHY

Have your day in the sun with this summer duo. A thin layer of light-sensitive dye applied within masked-off lines on a blank tote bag turns dark blue, revealing lighter areas where images of swimsuits are laid. Pretreated, light-sensitive fabric, exposed with a paper cutout of sunglasses, is sewn into the drawstring-closure sunglasses case.

WHAT YOU NEED TO MAKE A SUMMERTIME TOTE

1-inch-wide painters tape

blank canvas tote bag

copyright-free swimsuit clip art from the Internet

Lumi Inkodye UV fabric printing kit: Inkofilm ink-jet printable film, Inkodye Snap Pack sunreactive printing dye in blue, Inkowash detergent

ruler

gold paint pen

WHAT YOU DO

1. Using painters tape, mask off four 3½×3¾-inch rectangles in the center of one side of the canvas tote bag as shown in Photo A.

2. Download copyright-free swimsuit clip art to your computer. Resize the images to about 2×3 inches and convert the images to black-and-white or grayscale. Following manufacturer's instructions, print the images onto ink-jet-printable film. Cut out the shapes.

3. Following manufacturer's directions and working indoors on a protected surface, spread a thin layer of sun-reactive printing dye in each taped-off rectangle on the tote bag as shown in Photo B. Use a paper towel to blot off excess dye from the tote bag if needed.

4. Lay swimsuit shapes on tote bag, in each taped off rectangle as shown in Photo C.

5. Lay tote bag in direct sunlight outdoors for 5 to 10 minutes. Take bag indoors and remove swimsuit shapes.

6. Following detergent manufacturer's instructions, wash tote bag to set the design. Dry the bag on low setting; press with a warm iron if needed.

7. Using a ruler and gold paint pen, draw a frame around the edges of each rectangle of the printed design.

SO-CUTE SUNGLASSES CASE

Print copyright-free sunglasses clip art onto paper; cut out. Fold an 8×9-inch piece of sun-reactive cotton fabric, such as raspberry cyanotype cotton, in half lengthwise; finger-press and unfold. Lay fabric right side up outdoors in direct sunlight and quickly lay sunglasses shape above finger-pressed line. Leave in sun 10–15 minutes to complete sun printing. Immediately run water over fabric until it runs clear; gently wring. Lay flat to dry or dry on low heat in dryer; press. Lay fabric right side down. Fold one 8-inch edge under ¼ inch; press. Fold edge under another 1 inch; press. Unfold 1-inch edge. Lay a piece of cord for drawstring along the 8-inch edge and fold fabric, encasing the drawstring between the fabric layers. Sew the folded edge in place, being careful not to catch the drawstring in the stitching. Fold fabric in half lengthwise, right sides together. Sew along short and long edges, stopping before drawstring openings. Turn right side out. If desired, make tassels from embroidery floss and use the cord ends to tie floss bundles. Wrap each bundle with embroidery floss; knot and trim tassels.

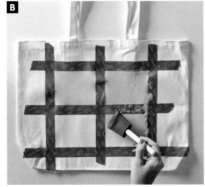

Do It for Dad

Cast artistic concrete projects to surprise Dad on his special day in June.

PENCIL IT IN

A stylish, industrial pencil holder makes for a clutter-free desk. Set 3 large copper pipe couplings upright on plastic sheeting. Mix 2 cups concrete mix with 2 teaspoons of one shade of ultrafine pigment, then mix 1 cup of concrete with a second shade of ultrafine pigment. Stir chilled water sparingly into each mixture until concrete develops the consistency of pudding. Combine both mixtures and lightly swirl together. Pour concrete into each of the large couplings. Cut out small circles from plastic sheeting and wrap one end of the 3 small copper couplings so they don't fill with concrete as they are inserted into the wet concrete. Let dry for 24 hours.

TO THE LETTER

A concrete letter bookend will add a monogrammed touch to Dad's shelf. Cut out the back of a hollow cardboard crafts letter with a crafts knife. Mix 1 cup of concrete mix, such as Buddy Rhodes Artisan Concrete Mix, with 1 teaspoon of ultrafine pigment (such as Buddy Rhodes) for each of the two mixtures. Stir chilled water into each mixture until concrete develops the consistency of pudding. Combine both mixtures and lightly swirl together. Pour mixture into the letter form and gently tap the mold on a flat surface to remove air bubbles. Let dry for 24 hours, then peel off the cardboard.

QUICK CONCRETE PLANTERS

Showcase botanicals in contemporary planters cast from vinyl concrete patcher. Select 2 plastic containers: one large, one small. Punch or drill a ¼-inch hole through the bottom of the small container. Attach a dowel to the large container's interior with double-stick foam tape as shown in Photo A. Smooth oil-base modeling clay where the dowel meets the large mold to create a watertight seal. Liberally coat the dowel, the interior of the large container, and the exterior of the small with petroleum jelly. Feed the small container onto the dowel.

Slowly add 4 parts dry vinyl concrete patcher to 1 part water, stirring until it resembles thick brownie batter. Fill the large container partway by scooping in the mixture, then tapping the bowl on the table to remove air bubbles. Continue filling until mixture almost reaches the small container's rim. Tap again. Smooth the surface with a gloved finger as shown in Photo B. Weight down the small container with pebbles; let dry 24 hours. Release the cast from the molds and remove the dowel, tape, clay, and pebbles. Gently smooth the planter's rim with 200-grit sandpaper. Finish the rim with gold leaf if desired.

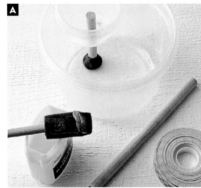

Hooray for the Red, White, and Denim Blue

With the addition of red and white accents, repurposed denim jeans transform into Fourth of July decorations worthy of oohs and ahhs.

AMERICANA STYLE

Square plate chargers are practical portable trays for picnics. For Independence Day, trim one side with a simple denim flower. Trim a side seam from jeans for the stem. Cut three leaf shapes. For the flower, cut a 1½×12-inch strip from denim. Sew a running stitch along one long edge; pull snug to gather and knot. Sew the ends together. Use a red or white button for the flower center. Adhere the denim pieces to the charger using quick-bond glue. Or, for temporary hold, use strong double-sided tape.

PERKED-UP PLATE

Jazz up square paper plates with a single snippet of denim. Cut a ¼×5-inch piece of fabric. Use a paper punch to make two holes in the corner of a plate, thread through the denim strip, and knot on the top.

PATRIOTIC PAILS

Create fun favors using denim scraps. Cut ¼×3-inch pieces of denim and tie onto the handle of a small pail to completely cover the handle. Fill the tiny buckets with red, white, and blue candies.

POCKET PROTECTORS

Cushion beverage glasses with coasters made from the back pockets of jeans. Trim around the pockets, cutting through both layers. Leave the bottom layer attached for extra absorption. Trim a corner of the pocket with buttons. If more protection is desired, cut a piece of cork to slip inside the pocket. Remove the cork and these coasters can be tossed into the washer and dryer.

RAGS TO RICHES WREATH

A flat wreath form gets a frilly facelift with camouflaging denim strips. Cut approximately 1×7-inch strips from jeans. Tie strips onto wreath to cover form. Add a red and white ribbon bow at the top.

A Way with Centerpieces

Craft glorious containers to show off summer blooms.

NATURAL WONDER

Embellish a wide-mouth round or square glass vase with natural images for a look both sweet and graphic. Make color copies from nature or botanical books; cut out each image using scissors or a crafts knife. Avoid color ink-jet copies, which can run when decoupage medium is applied. One at a time, apply decoupage medium to the front of each image as shown in the close-up photo. Secure it to the inside of the clear vase, layering images for a cohesive look. When dry, mask the outside of the vase with paper and spray-paint inside the vase (over the images) to create a consistent background color. To protect the finish, place a smaller watertight container inside the painted vase to hold flowers.
TIP: Shop for simple square and cylindrical vases at crafts and hobby stores. Before you buy, test that you can comfortably fit your hand inside the vase.

BRIGHT AS A FEATHER

Place a piece of silver duct tape on a cutting mat, then use a utility knife to cut out a feather shape. Peel back and position on a ceramic vase for an unexpected detail.

MARBLE MASS

A striking centerpiece of DIY painted pots delivers big impact on a low budget.

WHAT YOU NEED

plastic gloves
assorted sizes of terra-cotta pots and saucers
base coat spray paint in flat white or a light color
large plastic tub that can get messy
assortment of blue and green spray paints
paint stir sticks
cardboard or brown paper for drying

WHAT YOU DO

1. Work in a well-ventilated work space and put on gloves.
2. Spray pots and bases with base coat spray paint to thoroughly cover; let dry.
3. Fill tub about halfway with water.
4. Choose a few spray colors and lightly spray surface of water with two or three colors in a few spots.
5. Use stir sticks to lightly swirl the paints until they create a marbleized pattern.
6. Pick up dry painted pot and quickly dip into the water and pull out.
7. Place on cardboard or protected paper surface to dry.
8. Continue with additional pots, adding fresh paint and occasionally changing water if making larger quantities of pots and bases.

A Leg Up

Search flea markets, thrift stores, and your own garage for sturdy wooden ladders to make smart furniture and organizers.

OPEN CONCEPT

Ladder sections take sides when you build this freestanding shelf that beautifully blends old and new.

WHAT YOU NEED

vintage wooden ladder
circular saw
sandpaper
five 1×12×30-inch pine boards
paint primer and paint
paintbrush
tape measure
pencil
drill
countersink drill bit
3-inch construction screws
two 1×3-inch strip of salvaged wood
      (length varies by project)
1½-inch screws
miter saw

Note: You may purchase two smaller ladders instead; however, ladder rungs must align perfectly for even shelving.

WHAT YOU DO

1. Cut the ladder into two equal sections using a circular saw. Be sure ladder rungs align perfectly when two halves stand together. Sand the raw edges.

2. Cut 1×12-inch pine boards for the shelving. Ours are 30 inches long, but they may be any length. Sand, prime, and paint all sides. Lay both ladder sections flat. Measure and mark parallel points 4 inches to the right and left of the center on each rung. Drill holes at the marks using a countersink drill bit. Lay one ladder section on its side, center a shelf next to the top rung, and attach through the holes using 3-inch construction screws as shown in detail photograph.

3. With a partner's help, carefully stand up the ladder and attach the other ladder section to the shelf. Place a 1×3 strip of salvaged wood diagonally across the back of the unit. Strip should be long enough to diagonally connect the bottom of one ladder to the top of the other. Drive a 1½-inch screw at the bottom. Check that the shelf is level; attach the opposite end of the brace. Install the remaining shelves. Further secure the brace to the shelves. Place a second brace across the back. Mark and remove the section where the brace crosses the first diagonal board using a miter saw. Attach the brace. Trim overhanging brace ends.

TIP: Use construction screws to attach shelves to rungs. Their design prevents the wood from splitting when driven close to the shelf edge.

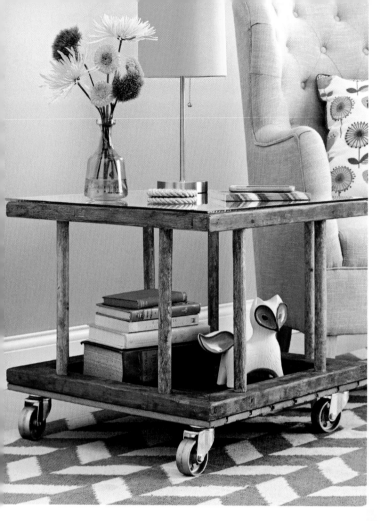

CHOP SHOP

Divide a long wooden ladder into four equal sections to build a one-of-a-kind side table.

To create table with two rungs centered in each section, cut each end of the sections with nonparallel 45-degree miter cuts. Stand the sections on their sides and fit the mitered ends together. Drill pilot holes at the corners of each joint with a 1/16-inch bit. Apply wood glue between the mitered ends; use corner clamps to hold the joints together as you hammer 3-inch finish nails into each corner, forming a box. Cut salvaged floorboards to create a base for the box and glue the planks together. Glue the box to the base and secure with 1½-inch finish nails. Sand all surfaces. To attach four casters to the bottom of the table, use a ¼-inch drill bit to make ½-inch-deep pilot holes; install the casters with ¼-inch lock washers and ¼×1-inch hex-head lag screws as shown in detail photograph. Apply a clear coat of finishing wax to the entire unit using steel wool. Wipe and polish with a clean towel. Place a ¼-inch-thick piece of tempered glass for the tabletop.

HANG DRY

With the right hardware, a ladder becomes a laundry room helper.

To prep the ladder for paint, sand it and wipe away the dust with a tack cloth. Prime the ladder and let dry. Paint the ladder with two coats of semigloss paint; let dry between coats. Once dry, measure 6 inches in from one end of the ladder and drill a pilot hole on the inside of the ladder. Twist a No. 104 2⅛-inch zinc-plated screw eye into the hole. Repeat on the other end of the same rail. To hang the ladder, use a stud finder to locate wall studs. On the rail opposite the screw eyes, mark hole locations to align with the studs. Using a countersink drill bit, drill holes through the rail at each stud. Attach the ladder to the wall by inserting 3-inch screws into the studs. Extend about 2 feet of steel chain (rated for the necessary weight capacity) from the screw eyes to the wall at a 45-degree angle and mark the wall. With a drill bit, make a ½-inch-deep hole into each mark and screw in No. 104 2⅛-inch screw eyes. Connect the chain from the screw eyes on the ladder as shown in the detail photograph. Trim excess chain as necessary using a rotary tool or bolt cutter or remove extra links with pliers.

STEP RIGHT UP

Give a 3-foot stepladder new life as a countertop plant stand.

To remove the metal side braces and back legs of the ladder, drill through the metal rivets. Next, measure the width of each step and cut three 1×8 pine boards to size. Sand the ladder and shelves. Use a countersink drill bit to make a hole in each corner of the underside of each step. Smear wood glue on the top tread, align the top shelf with the back of the tread, and secure from below with a 1¼-inch screw in each pilot hole. Place the ladder against the wall to determine the placement for the next two shelves (the back of the shelves should rest against the wall); glue and screw the shelves in place. Apply two coats of antique nickel spray paint; let dry between coats. To attach the unit to the wall, install a 1×2 pine ledger board with 2-inch screws just below the top step. Secure the shelf to the ledger board from the top using 2-inch screws.

Pillow Perk Up

Enhance decor with colorful toss pillows.

TO DYE FOR

Washes of fabric dye and chalk paint flow across once-plain linen cushion covers in loose, freeform style.
Follow the manufacturer's directions for applying dye and paint to fabric. The bottom cover was folded in half, dipped at the fold line into a bath of kelly green liquid dye, rinsed, and dried. A solution of four colors—emerald, kelly green, dark green, and teal—was brewed to create its broad band of green at one edge. Immerse the opposite edge into a watery bath of pink chalk paint. For the middle pillow cover, dip one end in emerald dye for 10 minutes, then slowly lift and hold it in short increments for an ombré effect. Apply bands of watered-down yellow and pink chalk paints using a paintbrush. The top cover uses the same techniques in different intensities.

SITTING PRETTY

Vintage accents add feminine charm to purchased pillows.
Cut doilies as needed to fit a pillow or wrap them around to the
back, securing with spray adhesive. Use fabric glue to secure
pom-pom trim around a pillow. The piping on this round pillow
helps conceal the glued seam. Add a vintage flower pin or
other embellishment at the center.

GO GRAPHIC

Felt pieces and embroidery floss accents dress up plain pillows for a stunning effect.

For the prismatic pillow cover, cut triangles from gray, cobalt blue, and teal felt. Attach them to a white throw pillow cover with fabric glue or iron-on adhesive. Highlight the shapes with long stitches in coordinating embroidery floss as shown in the detail photograph. For the diamond pillow cover, cluster white felt diamonds in one corner of a gray pillow cover, then disperse them outward to suggest a supernova. Using the photograph for placement guide, attach the felt diamonds using contrasting embroidery floss in long and short running stitches as shown in the close-up photograph. Running stitch diagram on page 152.

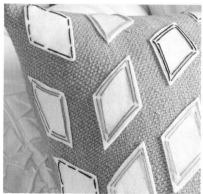

Hankie Swanky

WINNING EDGE

Layer a premade pillow with vintage flair. Cut off the point of a clean, pressed decorative handkerchief. Press under the raw edge. Handsew the diamond shape to the top of the pillow using coordinating embroidery floss and running stitches. Running stitch diagram on page 152.

PRETTY PIECE

Save the best part of a handstitched hankie to create a graceful bookmark. Cut the fabric strip and gently fray the unsewn edges. For stability, use an iron to bond a piece of heavy fusible interfacing to the back.

LOVELY LINER

Pure white initial handkerchiefs make charming basket liners. Bleach the hankie with a mild solution, rinse, and wash as usual. Press the clean fabric flat. Place the handkerchief in a basket, draping the decorative corner over the edge.

OLD-FASHIONED CHARM

A bouquet looks extra special accented with a decorative hankie. Fold the handkerchief in half, points together. Tie the ends around the neck of the vase.

GRACEFUL GREETINGS

A dainty handkerchief print does double duty gracing the front of a notecard as well as its envelope. To make the card, cut a rectangle from a piece of adhesive-back cardboard to fit a notecard as shown. Cut a piece from the handkerchief that is ¼ inch larger on all sides. Center and adhere the cardboard to the back of the handkerchief piece. Tape the edges to the back. Use double-sided tape to mount the handkerchief piece to two layers of cardstock, trimmed to frame fabric. Mount on notecard. Use double-sided tape to adhere a corner of the handkerchief to the envelope flap. Do not mail if envelope is embellished as shown.

boo!

TREATS ALL AROUND
Silly, scary, or scrumptious, Halloween is about to become eerily unforgettable.

Terrifying Tabletop

A few unexpected touches on the dining table put everyone in the Halloween spirit.

THE EYES HAVE IT

Guests will do a double-take when they see something staring back at them from their place at the table. Nestled in a grouping of dried roses, the realistic eye is actually a spray-painted marble.

WHAT YOU NEED

1-inch-diameter circle punch
cardstock scraps
large white marble
small key ring, washer, or bottle cap
spray paint in mint green and black
large circle paper punch
small cloche
moss
clean dried or faux roses

WHAT YOU DO

1. To make an eye, punch a 1-inch circle from cardstock, making it as far from the paper edge as possible as shown in Photo A.

2. In a well-ventilated work area, set the marble on a key ring, washer, bottle cap, or other small round object to keep it from rolling. Place cardstock piece over the marble and spray-paint mint green through the opening as shown in Photos B and C. Let the paint dry.

3. Place the cardstock on the marble again, aligning the cutout with the painted circle. Use black spray paint to carefully spray around the edge of the circle opening, allowing the green to show in the center as shown in Photos D and E. Let the paint dry.

4. Use the paper punch to make a hole in another cardstock scrap, punching it as far from the paper edge as possible as shown in Photo F. Place cardstock piece over the marble, centering it in the green of eye, and spray-paint black through the opening as shown in Photos G and H. Let the paint dry.

5. Place a cloche in the center of a plate, remove the cover, and line the base with moss. Arrange roses on the cloche base. Gently open one of the flowers and set the marble in the center. Replace the cloche lid.

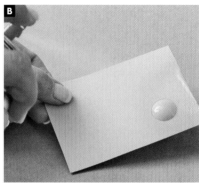

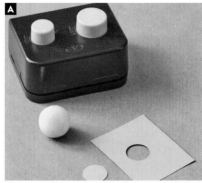

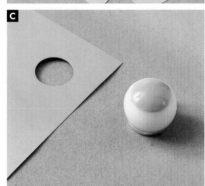

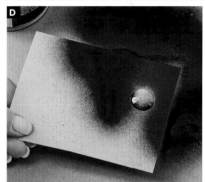

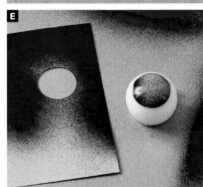

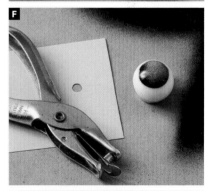

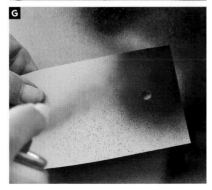

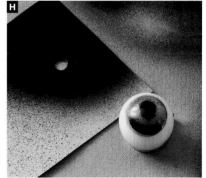

The Bewitching Hour

Fright night isn't complete without black cats, spooky faces, and glowing candles.

BLACK-AS-NIGHT CATS

On the table or on the floor, black cats add startling Halloween flair. Remove stems from a large and a small pumpkin and paint with black acrylic paint. Let dry. Trace patterns on page 153 and cut out. Use patterns to cut shapes from cardstock for ears, eyes, and a nose. Give both ears a rounded shape by curling edges forward. Fold back ¼ inch on bottom of ears and glue ears to top of small pumpkin as shown. Using glue, such as Beacon Magna-Tac 809, attach the eyes and nose; paint a mouth using white acrylic paint. Stack small pumpkin on top of large one. Place a spoon gourd painted black behind large pumpkin for a tail.

OWL PUMPKIN

Large pumpkins make playful no-carve owls. Trace patterns on page 154. Cut out patterns and trace on cardstock: a set of brows, two eyes, a beak, two wings, one each of body templates. Glue pieces together as shown (beak should be behind eyes and brows on top of eyes), then glue to surface of pumpkin. Tack down with pins and let dry. Glue wings to side of pumpkin and curved body pieces to the front. Tack and let dry.

CONJURED-UP CANDLES

Download Halloween designs from the Internet and print onto decal paper. Spray the front with two coats of acrylic spray, letting dry between applications. When decal is dry, cut around design and soak in a shallow dish of water until decal starts to lift from its backing. Carefully apply decal to candle, peeling off backing. Gently blot with a paper towel to eliminate air bubbles and excess water. Let dry for a few hours before handling.

TRICK OR TREAT CUPS

Wrap decorative tape diagonally around 12-inch lengths of floral wire. With an awl or hole punch, make a hole in each side of decorative paper cups. Thread wire through holes, turning ends up on the inside. If desired, embellish with pieces of ribbon.

SPIDER SENSE

Lanterns wrapped like mummies and a swarm of spiders team up for a spooktacular scene. To make each spider, use one 3¼-inch and one 4½-inch Smoothfoam half ball. Using a serrated knife, trim an equal-size sliver off one side of each ball. Gently stretch a long strip of black crepe paper around edges of each ball to cover. Adhere paper to the back with glue or tape. Make a hole in centers of flat sides of both the small and large balls with a needle. Insert a toothpick or piece of floral wire into hole of larger half and push both balls together to form the spider's body. Add a dab of glue between layers for extra hold. For the legs, bend eight 12-inch chenille stems as shown. Tape first set of legs to back of spider, just where the head and body meet. Tape additional sets of legs underneath.

MUMMY LANTERNS

Battery-operated candles are a must to this Halloween lighting. Cut strips of cheesecloth about 2 inches wide and long enough to cover a glass cylinder; secure one end to the cylinder and wrap. Don't aim for neatness; the idea is to create uneven layers like on a mummy. Attach loose ends with a dab of gel glue. Continue layering other strips and, if desired, embellish with mini safety pins. For safety, light only with battery-operated candles.

TREATS, NO TRICKS

Transform a tabletop with heaps of sweets surrounded by a menagerie of creepy critters and goblins. Rise to the occasion with decorations that elevate your efforts. To make balloons, print out letters, page 153, to desired size; cut out. Trace around templates onto the back of paper or paper-backed fabric. Cut out letters and spray with repositionable spray adhesive. Let dry for a few minutes, then adhere to a 6-inch round inflated latex balloon, positioning the middle O first, followed by the other letters. To make the streamers, cut five 5-inch-wide strips from 19×25-inch sheets of medium-weight drawing paper. Using scissors, make a series of cuts along the bottom, 1½ to 2 inches apart, stopping ½ inch below top edge. Rotate paper and cut between each of the existing cuts, again to about ½ inch below top edge, to create a zigzag effect as shown. Tape top strip in place on ceiling, and gently pull strips apart to form a streamer.

CANDY CREATURES

Bring on the sweets in containers that double as decorations. To avoid using excessive amounts of candy to fill big glass vases, place a drinking glass upside down in the middle of each. Download cat and owl templates and cut out; trace around templates onto colored cardstock and cut out. Glue faces together as shown. Attach to front of vase with double-sided tape. For owl's eyes, use circle punches or a circle cutter and pinking shears to create a decorative edge.

PUMPKIN SPIDERS

Paint mini and/or small pumpkins with black acrylic paint and let dry. Leave some pumpkins unpainted if desired. Using a metal skewer or nail, make four punctures just above the midline on each side of the pumpkin and insert black pipe cleaners. Use eight pipe cleaners per spider for legs; bend them to create knee joints and feet. Trim off excess. Adhere googly eyes.

ORANGE-AND-BLACK MAGIC

A pom-pom wreath and graphic paper pumpkins create a devilishly clever display. Make yarn pom-poms in various colors and sizes. Slip a U-shape floral greening pin through the tied yarn that holds pom-pom together and insert each pom-pom into a foam wreath form to cover.

PAPER PUMPKINS

Cut 12×12-inch cardstock into strips 1 inch wide and 9 to 12 inches long, depending on desired size. Make 20 strips for smaller pumpkins, 24 for larger. Punch a hole in top and bottom of strip, ¼ inch from the edge, making sure holes line up. Place a brad fastener through top hole of strips to secure. Repeat for bottom holes. Bend strips so that they form a backward C. Tie a piece of string in a knot around a brad. Pull string taut and tie around the bottom brad, knot, and trim. Separate strips into a sphere. Fold a piece of floral wire in half and twist each end around your finger to make tendrils. Twist tendrils around brad at top of pumpkin as shown. For the stem, twist a rectangle of crepe paper and flare the bottom outward like a skirt. Apply glue and adhere over the brad.

HALLOWEEN PILLOWS

Set the mood for an eerie evening by conjuring up a few wickedly wonderful embellished pillows. Use the pattern on page 154 to cut shapes from felt using the photograph as a color guide. Place patterns facedown on 12×18-inch felt sheets and trace with white pencil. Remove templates and cut out. Using a fabric glue, such as Fabri-Tac, adhere smaller pieces like cat's eyes to the larger pieces. Turn designs face down, spray with adhesive, and attach to the front of a plain pillow cover.

That's a Wrap

Hello, yarn and hot-glue gun. Wrapping pumpkins and gourds in vibrant yarn gives them a modern spin. Start with faux pumpkins and your handiwork will last well beyond this fall. Like traditional Halloween hues? Choose the yarn colors to go with your October decor!

Boo!

IN STITCHES
Hot-glue the end of yarn to the bottom of a gourd. Wrap until you've completely covered the gourd. Secure yarn with a dab of hot glue. Use a sewing needle to stitch Xs around the gourd in contrasting yarn colors.

WOVEN BURLAP
Measure and cut burlap to fit around a pumpkin. Fray edges by pulling a few burlap threads. Using a yarn needle, intermittently weave yarn horizontally through burlap. Repeat with assorted yarns. Secure burlap to the pumpkin using hot glue.

BRIGHTLY BANDED

Hot-glue the end of a piece of yarn to the center of a gourd. Wrap the yarn until you've created a color band 1–2 inches wide. Secure yarn with a dab of hot glue. Hot-glue the end of a contrasting piece of yarn to the center of the first color or beside the last color (as shown). Wrap the yarn until you've created a color band about 1 inch wide. Repeat as desired. Secure yarn with a dab of hot glue.

WEB DESIGN

Secure yarn to the bottom of a pumpkin with hot glue. Wrap in a random web design, using hot glue to secure if needed. Repeat with assorted yarn colors, wrapping randomly atop one another until web design is created.

TOTALLY TASSELED

Secure yarn to bottom of a pumpkin stem with hot glue. Tightly wrap yarn up the stem, securing with hot glue when needed. Clip yarn at top and secure. Tie five 8- to 10-inch strands as one around the base of the stem and knot. Fray edges.

Cut It Out

Paper decorations are delightfully frightful and wickedly easy to make.

SLITHERING SNAKES
Round the edges of a two-sided metallic posterboard, then free-form cut it in a spiral. Use then pattern on page 157 to cut a cardstock paper head; glue a notched ribbon tongue in place. Hang with string or wrap the snake around furniture.

COOL RECEPTION

Send a shiver up guests' spines with spiders scaling the walls and snakes dropping from the ceiling. Use sticky putty to hold the spiders to the wall.

DARK HARVEST
Create paper pumpkins from party-store corrugated lanterns and honeycomb spheres. Dust them with gold and bronze spray paint for an other-worldly glow and attach paper leaves cut from the pattern on page 156. Make scrolling vines using our spiral-cut snake technique.

RING OF FIRE

Cut 5-inch squares from six colors of gray and black tissue paper. Make a stack of five or six, twisting slightly from the centers. Secure to a foam wreath with a U-shape florists pin; repeat. Keep the bottom and inside clear so the form sits level.

FEATHERED FOES

Chilling ravens perch atop doors and windows to heighten Halloween decor. To make these trace-cut-fold ravens stiff enough to stand, glue together 2 sheets of black cardstock before cutting out using the patterns on page 156. Secure each bird's folded base to the surface using glue dots or double-sided tape. A hole-punched eye eerily follows guests around the room.

PUMPKIN PATCH

Mix-and-match pumpkins or gourds in a variety of colors, textures, and perfectly imperfect shapes to fashion a tablescape that will last through Thanksgiving. Affix paper leaves and vines (see patterns on page 156) as used for the paper pumpkins on page 134.

ALL AGLOW

Haunt your tabletops with a village of easy-to-assemble paper-house luminarias. Use the patterns on page 158 to cut out each house shape. Tape vellum to inside and fold shape to make house; tape together. Place the house over battery-powered tea lights. Craft the luminarias from various textured papers for added interest.

Spooky Nibbles & Sips

This frightening fare will give your guests thrills and chills of the very best kind!

CARAMEL
POPCORN
BALLS

CARAMEL POPCORN BALLS

The combination of salty, sweet, chewy, gooey, and crispy is frighteningly irresistible! If you don't want to pop the popcorn, buy a bag or two of readymade—salted or unsalted, whichever you prefer.

WHAT YOU NEED

2½ tablespoons vegetable oil
1¼ cups popcorn kernels (unpopped)
¼   cup butter
1   cup packed light brown sugar
½   teaspoon salt
½   cup light corn syrup
⅔   cup sweetened condensed milk
½   teaspoon vanilla extract

WHAT YOU DO

1. Preheat oven to 200°F.
2. Heat 1 Tbsp. oil in a 4-qt. saucepan over high heat. When oil is hot, add ½ cup popcorn kernels and cover pan, swirling and shaking pan constantly. When corn stops popping, remove from heat. Transfer popped corn to a deep roasting pan or large metal bowl and keep warm in oven.* Repeat with another Tbsp. oil and ½ cup popcorn kernels, then make a last batch with remaining ½ Tbsp. oil and ¼ cup popcorn kernels.
3. In a saucepan, with a candy thermometer inserted, stir together butter, sugar, salt, and corn syrup; bring to a boil over medium heat. Stir in condensed milk. Simmer, stirring constantly, until thermometer reads 238°F. Stir in vanilla.
4. Pour caramel over popped corn and stir to coat. (The caramel is very hot, so be careful. Use a lightly buttered spatula to stir and get all the popcorn coated before using your hands.) Butter hands lightly; shape popcorn into balls 3½ to 4 inches in diameter. Makes 20 servings.
*Note: The caramel adheres better to warm popcorn, so don't skip this step!

BLACK HALLOWEEN PUNCH

BLACK HALLOWEEN PUNCH

The frozen floating hand adds an eerie touch to this dark and fizzy punch—and keeps it cold too!

WHAT YOU NEED

    Disposable thin latex gloves
    (unpowdered)
1   0.13 to 0.15-oz. envelope
    unsweetened grape soft drink mix
1   0.13 to 0.15-oz. envelope
    unsweetened orange soft drink mix
2   cups sugar
3   qt. cold water
1   liter ginger ale, chilled

WHAT YOU DO

1. To make a frozen hand, rinse out a disposable glove, fill it about three-fourths full with water, and seal with a rubber band. Lay flat on a baking sheet and freeze until hard, about 8 hours.
2. Stir soft drink mixes and sugar into cold water until dissolved. Combine with ginger ale just before serving. Dip frozen hand briefly in warm water, then peel off glove.* Float hand in punch bowl. Makes 32 servings.
*Note: If glove doesn't peel off immediately, dip it very quickly into hot water and cut it off instead of peeling. Make a couple extra as backups.

APPLE
TEETH
TREATS

CALZONE SNAKE

Stuffed with three cheeses (ricotta, mozzarella, and Parmesan), pepperoni, olives, green pepper, and mushrooms— all flavored with Italian seasoning—this slithering reptile will thrill and delight your guests. If you'd like, substitute 4 ounces of cooked and crumbled Italian sausage for the pepperoni.

WHAT YOU NEED
1   cup ricotta cheese
2   cups shredded mozzarella cheese
¼   cup grated Parmesan cheese, or to taste
1   4-oz. package thinly sliced pepperoni
½   tsp. Italian seasoning
½   cup sliced black olives (optional)
½   green bell pepper, cut into thin strips (optional)
½   cup thinly sliced fresh mushrooms (optional)
1   lb. pizza dough, thawed if frozen
1   egg
1   Tbsp. water

WHAT YOU DO
1. In a large bowl, combine cheeses, pepperoni, Italian seasoning, and, if using, olives, green pepper, and mushrooms.
2. Preheat oven to 375°F. Line a baking sheet with parchment paper.
3. Roll out dough into a long, flat strip about 6 inches wide and 20 inches long. Spoon filling along center of strip, leaving 1 inch space on all sides for sealing. Pull long edges of dough together and pinch tightly to seal, forming a long, filled roll. Transfer roll, seam side down, to baking sheet, arranging in an "S" shape, tucking ends underneath to seal. In a bowl, beat egg with water and brush egg wash over calzone.
4. Bake until calzone is golden brown, 30 to 35 minutes. Cool 5 minutes before slicing. Makes 14 servings.

APPLE TEETH TREATS
You can really use any kind of apples you like, but they should be at least 8 ounces each to make it easy to get wedges.

WHAT YOU NEED
2   Tbsp. lemon juice
1   cup water
4   Honeycrisp apples, cored and quartered
1   2.25-oz. package blanched slivered almonds

WHAT YOU DO
1. Stir lemon juice into water. With a sharp paring knife, cut a lengthwise wedge from the skin side of each apple quarter, leaving the peel around the wedge for lips. Cut the wedge wide enough to insert almonds into both the top and bottom. Dip mouths into lemon water to prevent browning. Poke 5 or 6 almonds into top and bottom of cut-out to make crooked teeth. Makes 16 servings.

CALZONE
SNAKE

BRAIN DIP

BRAIN DIP

To make this gross-looking but delicious appetizer even more realistic, weave thin strands of red and blue fruit leather between the cauliflower florets to approximate veins and arteries. It can be a little tricky, though, and whether or not it works depends on the anatomy (pun intended!) of your cauliflower heads. If the florets are tightly packed, it may make the heads fall apart. But if they are on the looser side, it should work just fine.

WHAT YOU NEED

2   heads cauliflower
     Toothpicks
2   cups guacamole (purchased or
     homemade)
2   cups salsa (purchased or
     homemade)
     Red and blue fruit leather, cut into
     thin strands (optional)

WHAT YOU DO

1. Remove all outer leaves from each head of cauliflower. Working with a sharp paring knife, carefully cut out stem and core, hollowing out just enough to shape a bowl, leaving outer head intact. Use toothpicks to hold the florets together if they fall apart.*

2. Set cauliflower bowls in shallow bowls (for stability) and fill with guacamole and salsa. Decorate brains by weaving thin strands of fruit leather between florets to resemble veins and arteries. Makes 12 servings.

***Note:** You may want to poke toothpicks into the florets right after you remove the leaves and stem, but before you tackle the core.

CHOCOLATE MICE

CHOCOLATE MICE

While these little creatures are kind of cute, using red candy beads for eyes does make them look diabolical! Plain chocolate wafer cookies are not available year-round in some supermarkets (just at the holidays). If you can't find plain wafers, buy chocolate creme-filled sandwich cookies and scrape out (and discard) the filling. Each half counts for one wafer cookie.

WHAT YOU NEED

4	oz. semisweet chocolate, melted
⅓	cup sour cream
1⅓	cups chocolate cookie crumbs (5½ oz., from approximately 24 wafer cookies)
⅓	cup powdered sugar
24	candy beads
¼	cup sliced almonds
12	(2-inch long) pieces of licorice string or laces

WHAT YOU DO

1. Stir together chocolate and sour cream in a bowl, then stir in 1 cup cookie crumbs. Cover with plastic wrap and refrigerate until firm, about 1 hour.

2. Roll level tablespoons of crumb mixture into balls, molding to a slight point at one end for the nose.

3. Roll "mice" in powdered sugar (for white mice) and in remaining cookie crumbs(for brown mice). Use candy beads for eyes, almond slices for ears, and licorice strings for tails.

4. Refrigerate until firm, about 1 hour. Makes 12 servings.

CANDY CORN
CUPCAKES

CANDY CORN CUPCAKES

Using a clever combination of orange and yellow cake batter and layering them in the paper liners gives the cake part of these treats the look of the candy corn topping.

WHAT YOU NEED

1 18.25-oz. package white cake mix
1 cup water
⅓ cup vegetable oil
3 eggs
4 drops red food coloring, or as needed
16 drops yellow food coloring, or as needed
2 cups prepared white frosting (from a 14-oz. can)
24 pieces candy corn

WHAT YOU DO

1. Preheat oven to 350°F. Line 24 cupcake cups with paper liners.
2. Combine cake mix, water, oil, and eggs in a bowl; beat with an electric mixer on low speed until thoroughly combined, about 2 minutes. Pour half the batter (2½ cups) into a separate bowl.
3. Color one bowl of batter orange by mixing in 4 drops of red food coloring and 6 drops of yellow food coloring. Color second bowl of batter yellow by mixing in 10 drops of yellow food coloring.
4. Spoon yellow batter into bottoms of prepared cupcake cups, filling each about one-third full. Gently spoon orange batter over yellow layers, filling cups about two-thirds full. Try not to jar or shake filled cupcake pans to prevent mixing layers.
5. Carefully put cupcakes into oven and bake until a toothpick inserted into center of a cupcake comes out clean, 18 to 22 minutes. Lift cupcakes out of pans and transfer to racks to cool completely, about 20 minutes.
6. Frost cooled cupcakes with white frosting, then top each with a piece of candy corn. Makes 24 servings.

MUMMIFIED JARS

Cheesecloth adds an eerie appearance to a plain glass jar. Add wiggly eyes and pipe cleaner snippets and you've created a monster. Use a paintbrush to coat the outside of a jar with decoupage medium. Wrap a piece of cheesecloth around the jar and trim off the excess. Brush another coat of decoupage medium over the cheesecloth-covered jar; let dry. Use hot glue to adhere wiggly eyes and pipe cleaner pieces. If using the jar for a candleholder, use only battery-operated candles.

Quirky Characters

Come haunting season, create Halloween characters to lurk around your home.

JACK AND JICK

Wide-eyed and full of smiles, this friendly pumpkin pair calls on recycled jars for bodies.

WHAT YOU NEED (FOR EACH FIGURE)

firm clear plastic ornament (one- or two-piece)
hot-glue gun; glue sticks
glass jar (or plastic weighted with sand)
yarn in burnt orange and flecked black
scissors
two 1-inch-diameter plastic rings
two ¾-inch brass grommets
two black buttons to fit inside grommets
felt scraps in black, orange, and other colors as desired for trims
toothpick
white acrylic paint

WHAT YOU DO

1. If using a two-piece ornament, hot-glue the segments together as shown in Photo A.
2. Hot-glue the ornament on top of the jar as shown in Photo B, positioning the ornament hanger inside the jar.
3. Place a dot of hot glue at ornament top to adhere end of orange yarn as shown in Photo C. Working in small sections at a time, wind yarn around in a circle, adding scallops of glue as needed to hold in place as shown in Photo D. Continue wrapping ornament until it is covered.
4. Hot-glue the end of the black yarn by the tail of the orange yarn. Wrap the jar with black yarn in the same manner as the head as shown in Photo E.
5. Gather components for eyes as shown in Photo F. Hot-glue the layers together as shown in Photo G. If desired, cut a pupil from black felt and glue in the center of the button. Dip the end of a toothpick in white paint and dot two highlights on each eye as shown in Photo H.
6. Cut out small facial features (nose, eyebrows, and smile) from orange felt; glue onto black felt as shown in Photo I, leaving room to trim a narrow border. Arrange and glue facial features to orange head as shown in Photo J.
7. For hat, cut a circle from black felt for desired rim and a 12×2-inch strip as shown in Photo K. Roll up strip for hat top and secure with glue. Glue the brim to the top.
8. Cut out a felt feather, approximately 1 inch longer than hat height as shown in Photo L. Fringe the edge and glue to hat. Glue hat to top of head as shown in Photo M.
9. For a bowtie, cut a 2×5-inch felt strip. Knot it in the center and trim ends if needed as shown in Photo N. Glue the bowtie to the character as shown in Photo O.

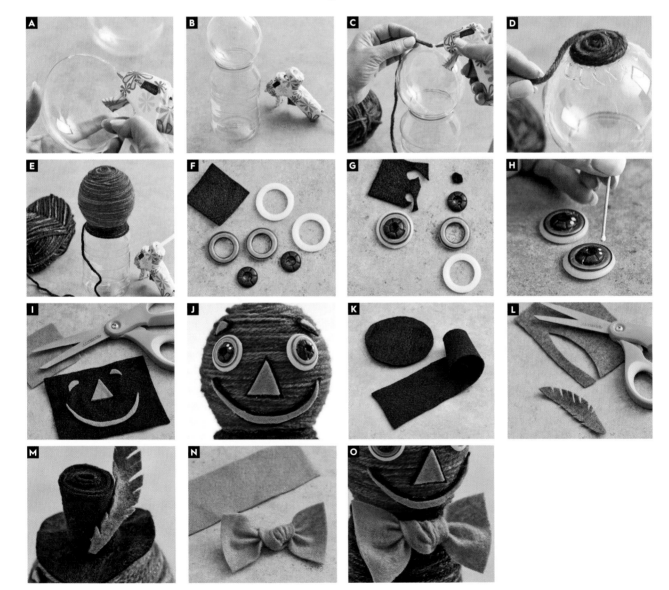

Boo!

TOO CUTE TO SPOOK
*All dressed up and everywhere
to go, this masked girl is ready to
trick-or-treat.*

WHAT YOU NEED
two 1¼-inch-long wooden split robin eggs
4-inch square beveled wooden plaque
wood glue
crafts glue
two 12-inch-long ¼-inch-diameter
    wooden dowels
drill and drill bits
2-inch-diameter wooden sphere
2½-inch-long wooden egg
two 1-inch-long wooden ladybug splits
fine-grit sandpaper
two ½-inch-diameter wooden bells
bamboo skewers
acrylic paint in pink, desired flesh tone,
    off-white, mustard, olive green,
    orange, aqua, avocado green,
    winter white, black, brown, burnt
    umber, light brown, red, light orange,
    metallic copper
artists paintbrushes
brown fine-tip permanent marking pen
clear acrylic spray
2-inch-tall wooden peg doll
1½-inch-diameter wooden disk
1¼-inch-diameter wooden knob with flat
    side
glass glitter in orange and black
scrap of chenille yarn in olive green
1 yard of ½-inch-wide black-and-white
    striped ribbon
sewing thread and needle
5-inch length of black 19-gauge wire
5-inch length of silver tinsel chenille stem

WHAT YOU DO
1. Referring to the photo and using wood glue, adhere two wooden split robin eggs for the feet side by side on the wooden plaque with narrow end of each foot pointing slightly out.
2. Cut each wooden dowel into 1-inch, 3-inch, and 8-inch segments. Using a drill bit slightly larger than the diameter of the dowels, drill a ¼-inch-deep hole into the 2-inch-diameter wooden sphere for the head. Dab wood glue onto one end of a 1-inch dowel segment and push the glued end into the hole in head for the neck; let dry.
3. Using the wooden egg for the body, drill a ¼-inch-deep hole into the narrow end of the egg and two ¼-inch-deep holes for legs approximately ¼ inch apart into the opposite end. Drill a ¼-inch-deep hole into

the top of each foot. Dab wood glue onto one end of each 8-inch dowel segment and insert glued ends into holes in bottom of body. Dab glue on other dowel ends and insert into holes in feet; let dry. Dab wood glue onto end of neck and insert glued end into hole at top of body; let dry.
4. Using a ⅛-inch drill bit, drill a hole approximately ¼ inch from one end of each 3-inch dowel segment for arms. Drill a ¼-inch-deep hole near the indentation on curved side of each ladybug split for hands. Drill a second hole through center of one hand where the pumpkin handle will go. Lightly sand holes. Dab wood glue onto undrilled end of each 3-inch dowel segment and insert the glued ends into the holes in hands. Let the glue dry.
5. Drill a ⅛-inch hole into each ½-inch-diameter wood ball. Cut two 1½-inch segments of bamboo skewer. Dab wood glue onto one end of each skewer segment and insert glued ends into holes in balls for hair buns.
6. Refer to the photo for all painting. Base-coat the head, neck, top of body, upper half of each leg, and lower half of each arm with pink; let dry. Paint same areas with flesh tone; let dry. Paint remaining areas of body and upper halves of arms with off-white. Paint base with mustard; let dry. Paint the feet and lower half of each leg with olive green; let the paint dry.
7. Using a pencil, lightly draw six elongated diamonds around body. Paint diamonds in alternating colors of orange, aqua, and avocado green. Paint multiple coats as needed; let dry. Erase visible pencil lines.
8. Paint off-white areas on arms and body with winter white. Paint a narrow aqua band near top of olive green section on each leg; let dry.
9. Paint a ¼-inch black band around tops of diamonds; let dry. Paint a narrow black band between off-white and pink areas on each arm; let dry. Paint shoes and lower half of base edges with black; let dry.
10. Drill a ⅛-inch hole through the body near the shoulder area.
11. Using pencil, lightly draw the hair, mask, eyes, nose, and mouth. Use a fine-tip brown marking pen to draw nose and mouth lines. Paint hair and hair buns orange; let dry. Paint mask black; let dry. Outline eyes, under mask, and around hairline with brown. Paint eye burnt umber; add light brown highlights. Paint lips red. Paint light orange circles on cheeks and knees.

12. Mark both sides of head for hair bun placement. Drill a ⅛-inch-deep hole into head at marks. Trim skewer on each hair bun to ¼ inch. Dab wood glue onto skewer ends and insert skewers into holes in head.
13. Lightly sand edges of wooden plaque. Spray entire figurine with clear acrylic spray; let dry.
14. For hat, paint wooden peg doll body with aqua; let dry. For hat pom-pom, paint the wooden peg doll head with black; let dry. Paint all sides of wooden disk black; let dry. Using wood glue, adhere disk to base of peg doll. Dab wood glue onto one end of a skewer; insert glued end into the hole and let dry. Trim skewer to 1 inch. Drill a 1-inch-deep hole at an angle into top of figurine head. Dab wood glue onto end of hat skewer and insert into the hole in head; let dry.
15. For jack-o'-lantern, drill a hole through the wooden knob, just below the flat area. Paint knob orange; let dry. Using brown fine-tip marking pen, draw the jack-o'-lantern face. Paint the eyes, mouth, and nose with mustard; let dry. Use burnt umber to shade the nose and mouth and to paint the pupils. Highlight the eyes with copper metallic. Spray jack-o'-lantern with clear acrylic spray; let dry. Brush a thin layer of white crafts glue onto the jack-o'-lantern, leaving the eyes, nose, mouth, and flat portion uncovered. Sprinkle orange glass glitter onto wet glue; let dry.
16. Brush a thin layer of crafts glue onto black portion of mask. Sprinkle black glass glitter onto wet glue; let dry. Repeat for hat pom-pom, hat brim, shoulder band, and black portion of shoes. Glue chenille yarn around hat for hatband.
17. Fold ribbon in half crosswise and stitch short ends together to make a ring. Stitch a gathering stitch across one long edge, leaving a long thread tail. Slip ribbon ring over head of figurine and pull tail to gather the ribbon around the body like a skirt; knot the thread ends.
18. Thread 5-inch length of wire through shoulder hole and holes in upper arms. Trim wire and bend each end into a loop to secure arms at the shoulders. Place a dab of crafts glue onto one end of tinsel chenille stem and insert glued end into one side of jack-o'-lantern; let dry. Thread the chenille stem through the hole in the figurine hand, dab glue onto the remaining stem end, and insert end into other side of jack-o'-lantern; let dry.

Light the Night

DAUNTING SILHOUETTE

Stage an eerie atmosphere with a raven silhouetted by flickering battery-operated candle. To add to the scene, wire a handful of gnarly sticks to the side of the lantern.

SO EASY IT'S SCARY

Dress up candle jars for the haunting season quicker than you can say "boo!" Apply a gemmed sticker to the jar and top with a coordinating ribbon bow.

ARACHNID INVASION

A battery-operated candle wrapped with pulled-apart gauze creates a frightful background for a spider gathering. Set the candle in a wide-mouth jar, allowing some of the gauze to drape over the lip. Arrange plastic spiders on the gauze and rest the lid on the top to give the eight-legged creatures an escape route.

DUNGEON STYLE

Chunky chain necklaces from a crafts store create a dramatic effect dangling from an orange pillar candle. Use short pins to hold the embellishments in place.

FRIGHT LIGHT

A small ornate picture frame makes a fun base for a Halloween candle. Spray-paint the entire thing black and let dry. Place a small candle on top of the frame and complete the look with a band of ribbon pinned around the candle.

patterns

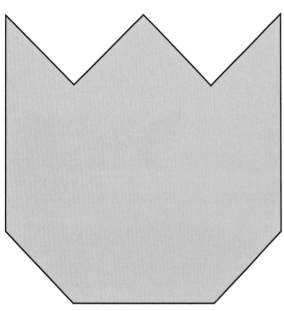

TULIP TIME
TULIP
page 25
Full-Size Pattern
CUT 3

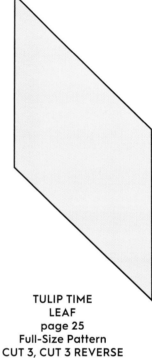

TULIP TIME
LEAF
page 25
Full-Size Pattern
CUT 3, CUT 3 REVERSE

Running Stitch

H
G

F
E

D
C

B
A

DOILY POCKETS
page 30

WINNING EDGE
page 115

GO GRAPHIC
page 116

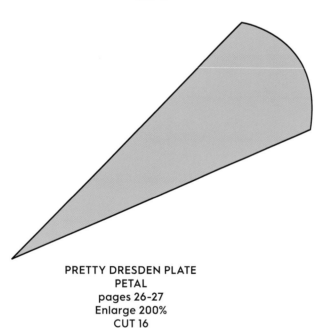

PRETTY DRESDEN PLATE
PETAL
pages 26-27
Enlarge 200%
CUT 16

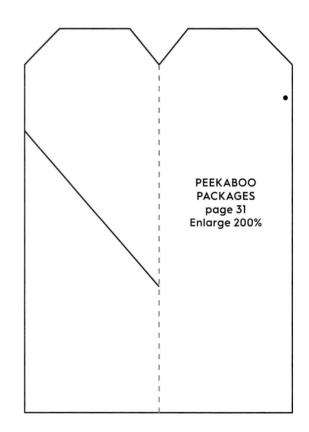

PEEKABOO
PACKAGES
page 31
Enlarge 200%

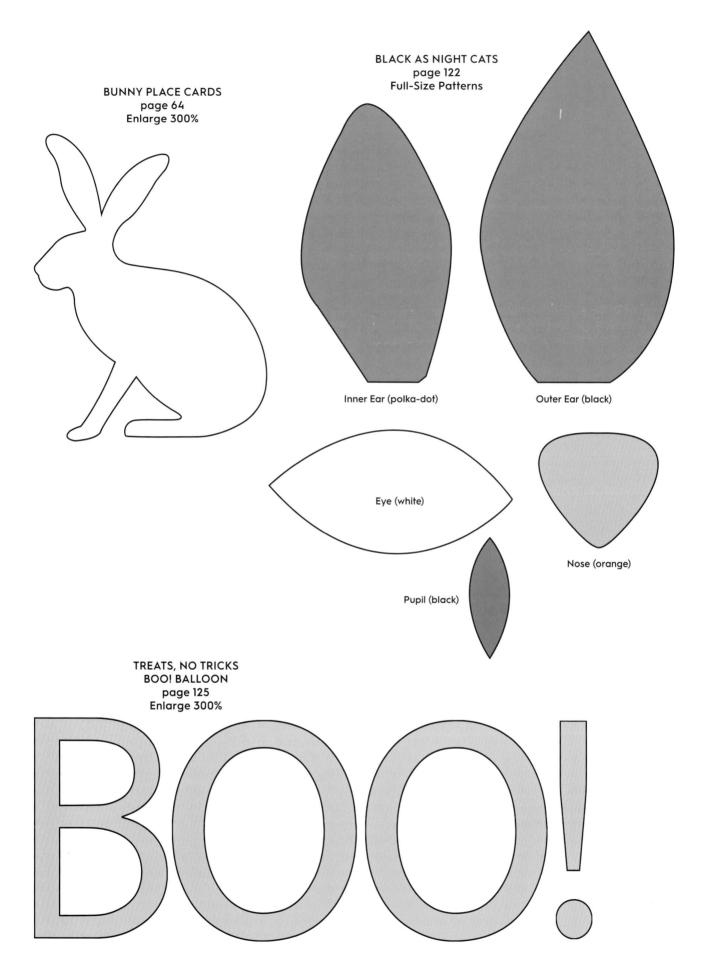

BUNNY PLACE CARDS
page 64
Enlarge 300%

BLACK AS NIGHT CATS
page 122
Full-Size Patterns

Inner Ear (polka-dot)

Outer Ear (black)

Eye (white)

Nose (orange)

Pupil (black)

TREATS, NO TRICKS
BOO! BALLOON
page 125
Enlarge 300%

BOO!

Patterns

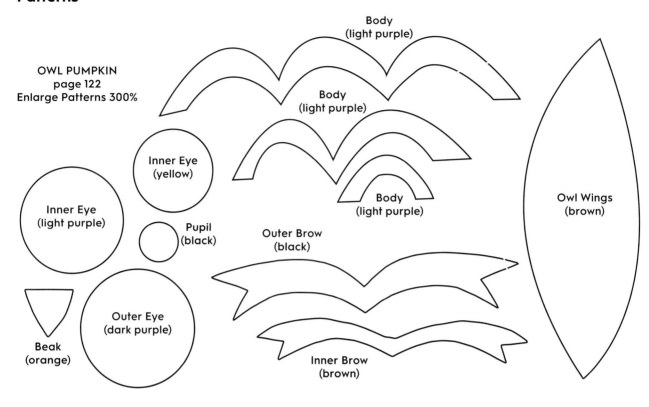

OWL PUMPKIN
page 122
Enlarge Patterns 300%

Body
(light purple)

Body
(light purple)

Body
(light purple)

Inner Eye
(yellow)

Inner Eye
(light purple)

Pupil
(black)

Outer Brow
(black)

Owl Wings
(brown)

Beak
(orange)

Outer Eye
(dark purple)

Inner Brow
(brown)

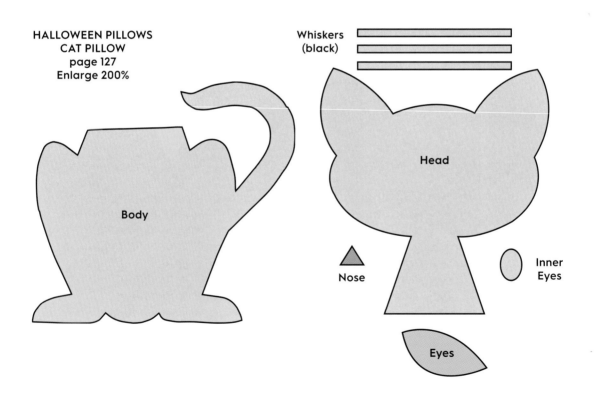

HALLOWEEN PILLOWS
CAT PILLOW
page 127
Enlarge 200%

Whiskers
(black)

Body

Head

Nose

Inner
Eyes

Eyes

HALLOWEEN PILLOWS
BAT PILLOW
page 127
Enlarge 300%

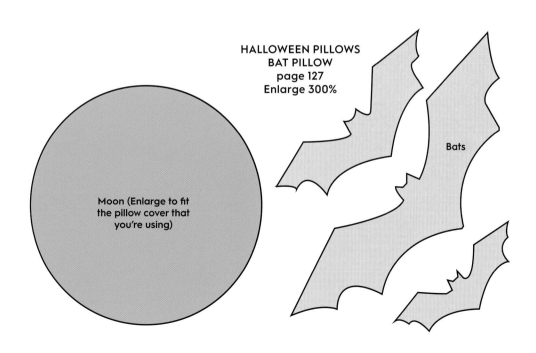

Moon (Enlarge to fit
the pillow cover that
you're using)

Bats

Patterns

CUT IT OUT
DARK HARVEST LEAVES
AND PUMPKIN PATCH LEAVES
page 134 & 136
Enlarge 300%

CUT IT OUT
DARK HARVEST VINES
AND PUMPKIN PATCH VINES
page 134 & 136
Enlarge 300%

CUT IT OUT
FEATHERED FOES
page 135
Enlarge 400%

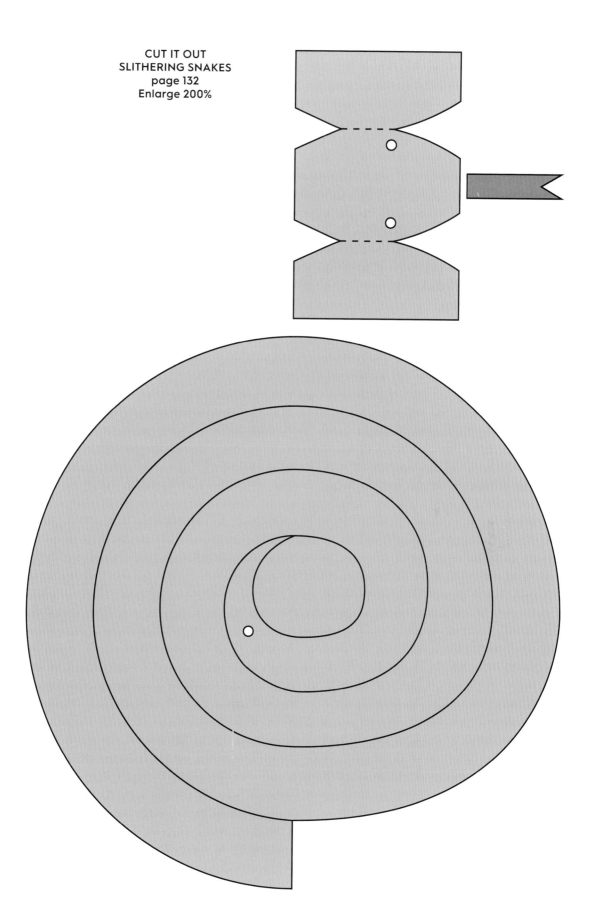

CUT IT OUT
SLITHERING SNAKES
page 132
Enlarge 200%

Patterns

CUT IT OUT
ALL AGLOW
pages 136-137
Enlarge 200%

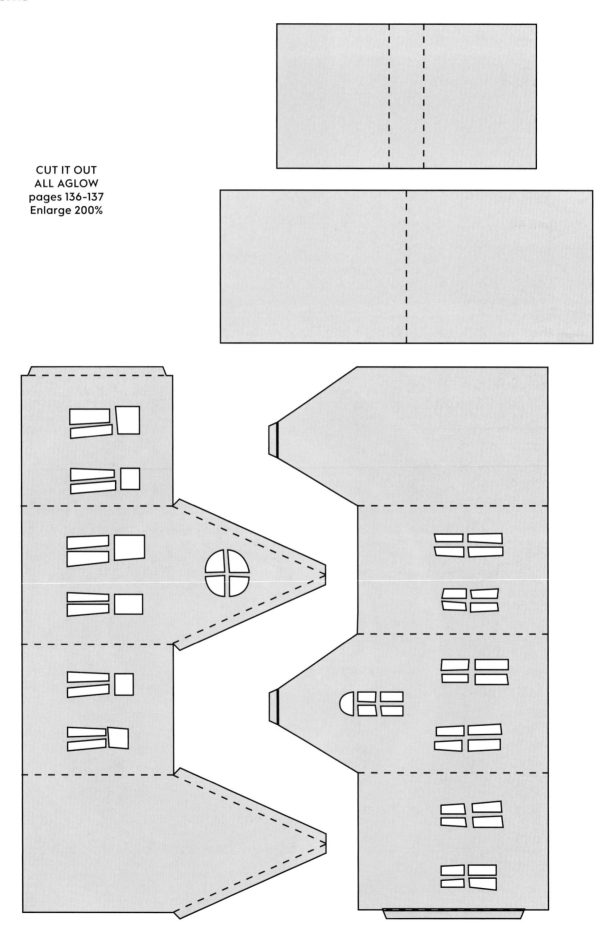

index

RECIPES

CREDITS

Photo Styling
Sue Banker
Doug Samuelson

Photography
Marty Baldwin
Jason Donnelly
Jacob Fox
Carson Downing